THE MANY FACES OF GRIEF

THE MANY FACES OF GRIEF

EDGAR N. JACKSON

Abingdon / Nashville

THE MANY FACES OF GRIEF

Copyright © 1972, 1973, 1974, 1975, 1976, 1977 by Edgar N. Jackson

Library of Congress Cataloging in Publication Data

JACKSON, EDGAR NEWMAN.
The Many Faces of Grief.
1. Grief. I. Title.
BJ1487.J29   242'.4   77-4363

ISBN 0-687-23203-1

MANUFACTURED BY THE PARTHENON PRESS AT
NASHVILLE, TENNESSEE, UNITED STATES OF AMERICA

To Jake and Mike

Contents

Introduction:
The Complex Emotion

Twenty years ago I was hard at work on a research project that was published under the title *Understanding Grief: Its Roots, Dynamics, and Treatment.*

That book was the first effort to make an organized and comprehensive study of grief as an emotion. My approach was psychological, and most of the resource material I had to draw on came from clinical studies in psychiatric and psychoanalytic literature.

Since that time a considerable body of research and writing has appeared that has broadened our knowledge of this widespread and painful emotion. But while the original ideas I explored have been examined in depth in more recent studies, the validity of my study has withstood the test of time and further research.

In lecturing to thousands of men and women in the care-taking professions, however, I have become aware of a need to understand the human aspects of grief as they are encountered in hospitals, funeral homes, and counseling rooms. It may well be easier to confront the dynamics of grief in theory than in the form of the baffling and often contradictory behavior of a person in the midst of a grief experience.

Therefore, I have tried to explore the nature of grief not so much from the point of view of the psychologist (who would examine its dynamics) as from that of a person who feels grief or observes at close range the grief of others.

I have long since lost confidence in the claims of empathy. For a time it seemed to be the favored obsession of counselors to think that they could in some mysterious way move into the feelings of others and, from that vantage point, therapeutically share a grief with greater wisdom and influence.

It seems to me now that the whole idea of an empathetic stance has something of the spurious about it. We know that no one can really feel the emotions of someone else—any more than he can see through the eyes of another, hear through the ears of another, or breath through the lungs of another. Any feeling is an intensely personal and quite private response to life.

The skillful counselor, or for that matter the friend or neighbor, needs to know that his most useful function is not to try to feel someone else's feelings but rather to give this someone else the full *right* to feel his feelings. The counselor is obliged not only to grant this right without restraint but to pay attention to the feelings of another so intently that they become the center of his concern and concentration. Then—and only then—is he apt to become the useful counselor who can wisely intervene to give healthful direction to someone else's feelings.

The dean of a medical school told me recently that one of the most baffling problems for the medical student was how to cope with the active emotions of the grief-stricken. Because of this frustration, in fact, the student was often inclined to recommend obliterating the emotions through use of sedation or tranquilizers, even though he might actually doubt this was the wisest course to pursue. If it were possible to understand the emotional content of grief more completely, the implicit threat felt by the medical student might be more easily managed and the treatment of the emotionally distressed person more wisely resolved.

It was with that purpose in mind that the present study has been pursued. And, rather than attempt to review the research and writing that has already been done by myself and others in defining and treating acute grief from the clinical perspective, my effort here has been to elaborate the many and varied ways in which this powerful human emotion manifests itself. Grief is a complex emotion. It is always personal. It is an extension of the inner life of a grieving individual. It reflects his values and his inner strength and weakness. It is significant behavior at a time when inner stress may be so great that other alternatives for managing life crises become inoperative.

In exploring these emotions in their many and varied manifestations, I have tried to identify not only the painful and distressing aspects of the behavior but also the creative and fulfilling ways in which grief may be used for personality growth.

It is my hope that by exploring the many-faceted expressions of grief, those who live or work with the grieving person may come to feel more comfortable and less threatened by what they observe, and may also be led toward more wise and useful intervention.

This exploration is essential, for we have learned through psychosomatic research that the repressed emotion or the unwisely met need may well be the point at which organic acting-out or illness moves into the life of an individual. Thus our greater understanding must not concern itself simply with knowing what is going on in the life of an individual; it must also ask how we may be useful in preventing some of the more devastating aftereffects of an unwisely managed emotional crisis.

To all those who have allowed me to observe and respond to their deep feelings in times of crisis, I give my thanks. Research with them has not been just a laboratory exercise. Rather, it has been an experience of walking together along the frontiers of life and among the outposts of human encounter.

1

Grief and Anger

Anger is often associated with grief. Angry behavior is often observed among grief-stricken people. It is reasonable to believe that anger, in one form or another, tends to be a component of the complicated emotion we call grief.

The anger that is an expression of grief can show itself in many ways. It can be direct. A week ago, a couple of miles from where I am writing, an accident touched off a display of anger. A tractor turned over, crushing the youth who was driving it. When the physician who rushed to the scene pronounced the victim dead, the victim's brother assaulted the physician. The expression of anger was so great that the physician had to spend the next few days in the intensive care unit of a hospital.

In this instance we would ask, Was the assault directed against the physician, or was some other force operative? It seems quite clear that the physician as a person or as a member of a care-taking profession was not the focal point of the irrational attack. Rather, because the physician was the one who announced the fact of death, he became the object of the explosive anger that was the initial response to the death.

This explosion of anger can show itself in other immediate and direct ways. It is often directed toward nurses in the hospital—as the persons closest to the event of death. Sometimes it is directed toward the clergyman—as one whose influence with the divine and the miraculous should

13

have been employed to prevent death. Sometimes it is directed toward the funeral director—as one who symbolizes death for the bereaved person.

There are times when the death of a parent lets loose a flood of angry feelings among the children. The sibling rivalries that have existed throughout the years but have never been effectively expressed may all be unleashed at once. One of the most graphic demonstrations of this rivalry may be the stormy conflict that surrounds the settling of an estate. At that time, great anger may be expressed over the possession of insignificant items charged with memories of early childhood.

I observed an angry display by a normally mature and well-controlled schoolteacher when a cousin came to remove the dining-room table that had been given to her by mutual agreement of all the relatives after the death of the mother. The schoolteacher threw herself on the floor and began to kick and scream. This table had been the center of family life when she was a child. The family ate together around it, studied around it, and played under it. Now, with the death of the mother, the home was being disorganized. The pain of confronting this new fact of life was so great that she felt abandoned. She became a little girl again for a few moments so that she could throw a tantrum and release her anger toward the parent who had, at this late date, made her an orphan.

Often the tense atmosphere of the funeral can be traced to the powerful feelings of anger that are a part of the grief. Among family members and relatives, many of the disturbed feelings of the past join with the events that affirm the changed circumstances of life (and the changed feelings that go with the events) to splinter family relationships and even cause divorce. The feelings of rejection that may have been diffused through the lives of the bereaved may be brought into acute focus by the event of death. This may make it possible for the accumulated anger of the past to take the overt forms that seem so often a part of the grief response.

The angry response to death may also be delayed, or it may be modified in such a way that it is difficult to recognize. A teen-age girl whose father died suddenly was angry at her father for dying, and she interpreted his death as a desertion. Shortly after his death, she became promiscuous—but with a strange and meaningful twist. After seducing a man, she would take him to the cemetery where her father was buried, then excuse herself for a moment, quickly return to the car, and drive off. She would never go with the same man twice. Thus, over a period of a couple of years, she left stranded in the cemetery quite a large number of men. It seemed that in her suppressed anger she was saying to the men she met—and indirectly to her father—that she could have any man she wanted, but she didn't really want any of them. In effect, she was saying, "You deserted me, Father. Now I will desert you symbolically through every man I meet."

Perhaps the same type of suppressed anger is revealed by the author of a book about funeral directors that appeared several years ago. The book is highly emotional and appears to have little concern for facts or accurate presentation of so-called research materials. The rather obvious explanation seems to be that the author suffered three tragic and untimely deaths under circumstances in which none of the usual therapeutic resources were available to help ease her grief. The anger appears to have snowballed through the years, then been unleashed upon those who are most readily associated with death—the funeral directors.

Several studies in recent years have linked physical violence, acts of vandalism, and delinquent behavior to anger that is related to the unresolved grief of those who have been the victims of trauma over death. Wherever there is ruthless and apparently meaningless behavior, it seems well to look deeper for its real causes. Geoffrey Gorer sees much vandalism as the acting out of anger against the injustice of society. In the case of the orphan, blame for the loss of the parent and the corresponding deprivation of emotional security is shifted from parent to society. Often vandalism is directed toward the institutions that serve as extensions of the parental image in society—the school, the church, the law, and the law enforcers. The relation here to anger and grief seems clear.

repressed anger stored up earlier in life. The spouse, because of the intimacy of marriage, becomes a focal point of response to frustration. The anger, therefore, is often shown through blaming another for the frustrations for which there must be at least a mutual responsibility. Often the anger is expressed by behavior that increases the frustration and compounds the anger.

Politicians know how to play on the frustrations of the electorate so that the powerful emotion of anger can be used for partisan purposes. Religious leaders have used the type of anger they call "righteous indignation" to accomplish their purposes, even when the intention has been to instigate religious wars—with all of their horrors.

If anger is so powerful a force, and if it can be used for such destructive ends, is there anything we can do about it? When death occurs and the reservoir of repressed anger is let loose in a grief response, is there something constructive that can be done about it?

Fortunately, the answer is yes. There are four steps we can take to help manage anger. First, we can admit it. Second, we can analyze it. Third, we can act it out. Fourth, we can abandon it.

Perhaps the hardest thing to do with anger is to admit that that is what it really is. We have been trained to cover up our anger so completely that we ourselves are fooled by the many and varied devices we use to hide it. But when there is a great amount of emotion directed outward or inward, it usually implies anger, and we might as well face it.

Once we have admitted our anger, we must lift it up to objective examination. Ask yourself, Why am I so upset? Does my attitude or behavior make sense? Back off and look at the anger to see if you can find out where the large burst of emotion for the small cause really came from. Has someone sat in your favorite chair or parked in your parking space? Has someone said something that stepped on your favorite prejudice or threatened your chance to make a little extra money? Has someone said something that came close to exposing some feeling that you wanted to keep hidden? Such questions open the way for an evaluation of your emotion.

The third step (having realized where the anger comes from) is to seek a wise and healthful way of working it out of your system. Do not suppress it further, for it will surely surface again. Rather, do something with it that will not hurt you or anyone else. Take a long walk, chop wood, play golf, or read a detective story. But know what you are doing and why—to get the full benefit from the acting out.

Fourth, make sure you believe that your anger is not worth what it costs in inner stress or fractured human relations. Anger can be a weak spot in your personality. It can complicate and destroy life. It isn't worth its price, so it should be abandoned for insight, understanding, and healthful action.

When grief triggers the reservoir of anger that life has stored up, it is well to recognize it for what it is and to work it through in creative and civilized ways. The funeral process can be a great resource for people who need to act out deep feelings in a way that is clearly understandable, yet socially valid. Anger is a part of life. The question is whether it will be used to become more destructive of self and others, or whether it can lead to creative insight and useful action.

2

Grief and Guilt

This week a funeral director from a western state called me and said, "One of my friends shot and killed a twenty-nine-year-old man who is the father of three children. He didn't mean to do it. He thought the man was a deer. But he feels terrible. He is overwhelmed by his guilt. Do you know of anything I can say or do to help this man?"

Often when death occurs there are overwhelming feelings of guilt and remorse. Almost always when death is confronted there are some feelings of guilt, although there may be no remorse. Even when you have waited and prayed for the kindly release from suffering that death brings, there may be feelings of guilt. This seems paradoxical, but it is true. What explains this paradox? What can we do about it? How can we help people who are suffering this painful emotion of guilt?

To begin with, we need to realize that guilt is a complex emotion. It is built into life through a long and complicated process. To be able to feel guilt is a sign of our capacity to feel with others. If we do something that hurts them, we can feel the hurt.

Guilt emerges at the point that social concern is felt. This usually begins to happen early in life. For example, when we are young, we are dependent upon parents for nearly everything. But we also have a will of our own and want to assert it. If we cannot do this when parents are watching, we sneak off and do it when they are not able to see. So we do things "behind the barn." We raid cookie jars and steal candy. While we may enjoy the forbidden fruits, they are never without cost; for we reap the fear of being discovered and the guilt that accompanies that fear.

As the growth process continues, there are other points at which guilt is discovered or developed. Sometimes guilt is cultivated by parents who say, "Aren't you ashamed?" or by institutions that keep reminding us of our sins so that we will have our guilt always before us. Guilt, therefore, is reinforced by agencies of social control that would use it to direct our behavior.

With adolescence comes the conflict between being dependent and being independent. The teen-ager knows that he expects his parents to provide the necessities of life. Yet he resents this dependence because he wants to be free to do what his strong life-impulse demands. The inner conflict leads him to do things he knows are against his parents' wishes; yet he continues to make the usual demands on them. His innate sense of justice makes him ashamed of his two-faced behavior, and he feels guilt.

Through the years there is a buildup of the capacity to feel guilt. This is healthy and important. Our whole system of law and order is founded on the assumption that human beings are creatures capable of feeling guilt, and that that guilt usually keeps them from injuring others or violating their rights.

However, there are times when it seems valid to a person to endure the pain of guilt in order to enjoy doing the things that he knows may injure or threaten others. So he goes hunting though he knows that firearms are always potentially hazardous. He drives after drinking though he knows his ability to handle a potentially lethal vehical is impaired. He says damaging things to protect himself even when he knows he is lying. And at each point he is apt to feel mild guilt as he "gets away" with his behavior—possibly much deeper guilt if he doesn't.

But guilt is not only complicated in its social origins and development. It is also an emotion that may show itself in different ways. There are at least three kinds of guilt. There is real guilt, where cause and effect relationships are obvious. There is neurotic guilt, where effect is out of proportion to cause. There is existential guilt, which is so deeply implanted in life that cause and effect seem to be irrelevant—guilt is felt because of a generally poor opinion of one's capacities, not because of any particular act or event.

Let us look more closely at these three types of guilt. Real guilt is the kind of guilt we see most often. When something you have done is a clear cause of injury to someone else, you usually have a clear and uncomfortable feeling of guilt. It may be an act as simple as bumping into someone in a supermarket and jarring a box of eggs out of his hands. You know you should have been watching where you were going. You accept some blame, immediately apologize, and offer to pay for any broken eggs. Here cause and effect are obvious. Here blame is easily assessed and accepted. In fact, the blame may be accepted and the offer of restitution made as a form of self-protection; for otherwise you would be subject to the judgment and implied reprimand of persons who may have observed the chain of events. The social status of the "witness" is an important force in creating feelings of guilt. So sometimes we blame ourselves first, in order to avoid social judgment by others.

But even though real guilt is a common form of the emotion, it is also true that we very often develop techniques for protecting ourselves from its burden. In moments of stress we say things that could hurt someone, then try to make light of it as if only making a jest. This is a form of apology that is designed to take some of the sting out of both sides of the exchange.

Sometimes we may seek to avoid the full measure of blame by passing on to other persons or events or even things the responsibility for what has happened. I caught myself recently doing just that. I was following another car too closely in heavy traffic on a wet and potentially slippery highway. When the car ahead of me stopped suddenly, I jammed on the brakes so rapidly that I started my car into a skid and slowly but irrevocably slid into the car ahead of me. I knew that I was legally at fault. I felt personally chagrined at being so careless a driver. While I admitted my responsibility to the other driver, I found myself making an excuse. "I didn't realize that the road was so slippery," I said. I was blaming the road for my own lack of skill as a driver. How quickly and easily we may do this and not realize it is a way of protecting ourselves from the burden of guilt.

Though we encounter real guilt most often, it may well be true that the other two types of guilt—neurotic and existential—may cause the most discomfort and distress in people's lives. So we will want to look more carefully at these more distressing, but often quite nebulous, kinds of guilt, to try to understand their impact on life.

Neurotic guilt exists when we feel more of the painful emotion of guilt than seems warranted by the circumstances. Sometimes we are aware of the fact that we feel more guilty than we should, and at other times we are not. In either case, it shows in the way we act; and because it can be distressing, it needs to be understood and (if possible) relieved.

Let us illustrate. Often the impulse toward self-punishment is related to neurotic guilt. Mrs. O. had been warned by her physician that she must give up her constant smoking of tobacco. She found this almost impossible to do, and finally she came into a counseling relationship to try to get help. She was a strong-willed person, able to exert control over her life in most other respects, but apparently helpless to cope with her drug addiction. During one session, in which we were trying to examine her deeper feelings, she blurted out, "All the time I feel like I want to burn my lungs out." After she had expressed this feeling, we were able to discover why she felt this way. She was engaged in behavior that was contrary to the basic value system she lived by. Her behavior was unacceptable to herself, but she felt strongly impelled to continue it. Naturally, she felt guilty about the whole thing; so she used her life-injuring addiction as a form of self-punishment. In this way she sought to reconcile her inner emotional battle. Her need to punish was so deeply rooted that she was quite unaware of the inappropriate cause-effect relationship until she discovered it rather painfully in a lengthy counseling process.

The National Safety Council has done extensive research on accidents. The premise was that an accident was a form of behavior that must have meaning. Usually an accident is referred to precisely as such, because the desire is to obscure the cause-effect relationship. When persons were questioned at length after an accident—in order to establish what their emotional state was just before it occurred—it was ascertained that in many instances the person causing the accident was experiencing a strong sense of guilt and apparently was desirous of inflicting punishment upon himself.

A young man whose father was domineering had a strong impulse to live his own life. He wanted to break with his home and his father, but the emotional control of the home had been so great that he was filled with an inner conflict that produced guilt. One evening he walked into a crowded bar with a toy pistol and said, "This is a stickup. Put it all on the bar where I can pick it up." In no time at all he was grabbed from behind by customers, and the police had to rescue him from the mob that was beating him brutally. The police said, "There is something wrong here. That guy knew he didn't have a chance of pulling it off." The inner conflict that produced the deep sense of guilt also apparently motivated him to seek the punishment he felt he needed.

A woman thirty-eight years old, in the hospital for her thirty-third surgical procedure, said, with a sense of satisfaction, "My surgeon has told me that I can have two more operations." Brought up in a very strict environment, she had been taught that everything having to do with sex was evil. In her married life she had found sex important and enjoyable, but there was always an aftermath of remorse and self-judgment. All of the surgery through the years had had to do with correcting functional disorders related to her sex organs. Her response to neurotic guilt appears to have been an employment of surgery as an instrument of self-punishment. Now she was saying, in effect, "I can go on enjoying sex for a while because my surgeon assures me that

I can have at least two more episodes of appropriate punishment." How much better it would have been if there could have been a direct attempt to correct the neurotic state that produced the disproportionate sense of guilt.

When a family was making arrangements for the funeral of an aged father who had died after a long illness, one son said, "I'll not have my father buried in anything but the best." The other members of the family said they did not feel there was any need for such expense, but they were overruled by the demanding son. The motivation here was quite clearly neurotic guilt. While the rest of the family had been routinely attentive to the father and his needs, the well-to-do son had not been able to take time from his ever-expanding career to come home to see his father. Now it was too late to make amends to the father directly, so he was going to do the next best thing as he saw it and punish his wallet. By demanding a large expense, he made it possible for himself to discharge his own personal obligation. As if in a court of law, he was pleading guilty to neglect and fining himself as punishment.

As these illustrations show, there are many and varied ways of expressing the guilt that occurs when cause and effect are blown out of proportion. This neurotic guilt can be a heavy burden, not only for an individual, but for the group within which the individual functions. How can such neurotic guilt be resolved? What better ways can be employed to resolve the guilt than the self-punishment that is often irrational and self-destructive?

Whether the neurotic guilt is conscious or unconscious, it is basic to the process of therapeutic release to be able to gain some form of insight that will make it possible for a person to see that he does not need to continue punishing himself. He can find more mature and more healthful ways of managing his conflicted feelings.

Insight can come about in many ways. Sometimes persons figure things out for themselves, though this is not apt to be the case. More often they benefit from creative communication with another person. Most often it is the professionally skilled person who helps them gain the perspective they need to free themselves from the impulse toward dangerous self-punishment.

Members of the care-taking professions are often aware of the acting out of unhealthy guilt. Doctors, lawyers, clergymen, and funeral directors observe the behavior that shows tendencies toward self-punishment. If they are able to gauge it for what it is, they may be able to help resolve the inner distress. Or, they may be able to guide individuals toward the services of those whose special skills can help significantly in working through the more damaging forms of neurotic guilt, that is, its self-injuring tendencies.

We have talked about real guilt and neurotic guilt. Perhaps the most baffling and difficult type of guilt to cope with is existential guilt. This is because it is more evasive as far as definition is concerned and also is more diffused through personality and society than we are apt to expect.

So first, let us try to define existential guilt. This form of guilt is rooted not so much in something you do as in something you are. It has to do with the basic problem of existence. Because we exist as moral beings, we live with expectations of life. Because we are creatures who are capable of self-judgment, we are often our own most severe critics. We say and do things that we regret and pass judgments upon ourselves for our behavior. When we examine our lives, we have a sense of our shortcomings and failures. Whenever we are confronted with death, we are reminded of the fact that life is short at best and man is mortal. Because he is mortal, he is limited. Because he is limited, he knows he will not be able to do the things he would like to do and feels he ought to do. So he feels guilty about being the sort of person he is.

Existential guilt is characterized by a vague sense of discomfort with one's self in the presence of personal failure. A person may say, "I'm sorry I'm this way, but its just the way I am." Or, after another moment of self-judgment, he might add, "I can't help it, I'm just a poor mortal." Existential guilt usually shows up as an effort to make an excuse for something that is beyond apology or excuse because it is not just a fault but rather a quality of being.

Existential guilt may show itself more through a sense of sins of omission than sins of commission. When a person has neglected a personal relationship, he may try to excuse himself by saying, "I just can't be two places at once" or "No matter how hard I try I can't seem to keep up with everything I am supposed to do." It is implicit in the old Pennsylvania Dutch saying "The faster I go the behinder I get."

Normally we would say that a person should not feel guilty because he is human and can't do everything he would like to do. The problem is that underlying the behavior of many persons there is this component of diffused and pervasive guilt.

It may show up in the form of projection when a person confronts death. It may lead him to say to another, "Poor Joe, he just never seemed able to make it," the implication being, "I am like Joe, and I will never catch up with life." And the older a person becomes, the more it seems that life rushes on, leaving behind its plethora of unfinished tasks.

Herman Feifel has pointed out that one of the major preoccupations of persons over fifty years of age, as it shows up in projective testing, is their own death. While it may not be expressed in conversation or conscious activity, it appears to influence the lower levels of consciousness. This is not surprising, because the older a person becomes, the more he is aware of the statistical factors involved in his life-span. He knows he is running out of time. This may affect his attitudes toward the death of any other person, for his grief is weighted with awareness of his own mortality and the diminishing of his own vital energies.

A major component in this awareness of the limitation of life seems to be related to existential guilt. While man has the urge for eternal or unlimited life, he has the deeply rooted feeling of inadequacy that accompanies his mortality. When he would aspire to the impossible, he is continually reminded that he is a creature of the possible, and this causes conflict.

When man confronts death in himself or others, he is dealing with an important part of his feeling of apprehension that centers on his existential crisis. This is the way things are, and he cannot separate himself from it no matter how much he tries. He is bound to confront physical death sooner or later.

When a person is confined in a hospital with a serious illness, he cannot easily avoid the thought that his existence may be coming to an end. He may be overwhelmed with the thought of all of the things he wanted to accomplish but did not. He may review in his mind, during the long and quiet hours of the night, his goals and his failures.

If he is hospitalized by a condition for which there is a clear correlation with carelessness and neglect, his existential guilt is apt to be compounded. Not only is he aware of his mortality, but he is also obliged to face his culpability in being unable to control his own behavior. I talked with a man yet in middle life who gasped out his words with difficulty as the life-preserving oxygen worked to sustain him. He had so severely damaged his lungs with smoking that the emphysema that assailed him had made him a cripple. He could not work, and his inability to work and the expense of his hospitalization placed a heavy drain on the family resources. But he said, "I know that the first thing I will do if I get out of here is to have a good smoke. I hate myself for it, but I can't help it." Here the existential guilt was bound up with his failure to manage a life-destroying addiction. But it was doubly distressing because he was aware not only of the human failure of control but of the natural bounds of his humanity that he was so carelessly trampling.

When the situation involves the death of another, the existential guilt may be just as active a force in life. We are bound to others by such a complex structure of human relationships that it is almost impossible to have been always wise and considerate. We get a different perspective on life when we look back across the broad sweep of it. We feel the emptiness of loss, but we also feel the sense of human failure that is apt to be a part of our feeling of fractured relationship to one another. Many of the things that are done at the time of death are efforts to resolve some of the aftereffects of our existential guilt. We pray, we invite others to make special prayers, we send flowers or other gifts, and we hope all of these varied efforts will allay in some measure the feelings of human failure that are so much a part of life and its relationships. There is so much more we would have wanted to do but did not do. There are so many more benefits we would have brought into life but failed to. Our limitations as human beings are paraded before the keyhole of conscious- ness with a relentlessness that is difficult to manage. And we are apt to be oppressed and depressed by our awareness of failure.

For many persons, the less manageable aspects of grief are those that assail us in the nebulous and not clearly defined areas of our existential guilt. Because we are not quite sure of what it is, we are not perceptive as to how to manage it. But becoming aware of its existence, developing courage to face it, and then generating the skills to manage it may not only reduce the impact of our grief but also make it possible for us to live with more discernment as we face the future.

It has often been observed that some persons seem to be broken down by their grief, while others grow to greater wisdom and strength through it. It may well be that it is at the point that a person develops skill in managing his existential guilt that he adds wisdom and incentive to his life. From then on he makes the most of each day as he lives it and communicates as much love and kindness to others as he can. From then on he knows how to measure his days and his human potential.

3

Grief and Loneliness

One of the most poignant forms of human suffering is loneliness. This is a desperate feeling of separation from those who give meaning to life.

Loneliness comes in a variety of degrees. Some of it is tolerable even though it is unpleasant, and some of it is so painful that it becomes actively or passively life-destroying.

In rural areas, electric companies rely on the persons they service to check their meters and send in the readings each month. If the meter is not read for two months, a staff member of the company visits the home of the errant customer to get a reading. One of the meter readers told me recently that although there is a five-dollar penalty for making the company representative come for a reading, there are some people who deliberately refuse to read their meter even though they are well able to do so. When I asked why this was so, my informant answered, "That's easy. They get lonely. Why, some of these old folks back in the hills seldom see anyone. They are glad to pay five dollars just to have someone come and pay them a little visit. They want to sit and talk all afternoon. I get to know some of these hill folks, and when they don't send in their reading, I know its time for me to have a visit with them again. Yes, people can sure get lonely back in the hills."

If people who do not have much money to spend are willing to pay a five-dollar penalty to have someone come and spend even a little time with them, we may begin to get some idea of how some people suffer from loneliness.

Recently I was working on a book manuscript and had to visit the office of the publisher. I had been writing something about the nature of human suffering and how to wisely cope with it. The woman who was doing the editorial work on the manuscript said one day, "I don't see anything here about my suffering. Why did you leave me out?"

At first I thought she was speaking in jest, for she was surrounded with other people in the office. She was well dressed and well groomed and seemed to be a pleasant and desirable person who should not want for companionship. She appeared to be in her late thirties and did not give the impression of wanting for anything in life. So I was puzzled and asked, "Just how do you mean that?"

She responded, "I wanted a career and I have my career. From nine to five my life is interesting and pleasant. I meet lots of remarkable people, but then there is five o'clock staring me in the face. I go home to my little apartment with my books, my records, and my loneliness. Years ago this was perfect for me. I liked it that way. But I began to realize I was tired of reading. I ran out of records that interested me. I was fed up with the stuff on TV. And now five o'clock comes like a nightmare. There are lots of women like me, and we really suffer, but no one seems to care."

I listened to her with sympathy and made a few remarks that were intended to be helpful, but she didn't take them that way. She blurted out her anger. "Everyone wants to put me off with some quick and easy answers. But I'm fed up with the superficial. I want something real out of life. To put it in its simplest terms, I want someone in this world to care whether I come home at night. Do you know what it is like to walk out of an office at five and not have any other one person on earth care whether you exist until nine the next morning, when you start doing the same old things all over again? No, you really don't. You tell me about your home and your family, and I have to work hard to keep from hating the whole picture. The quiet gnawing pain of unending loneliness going on until I die is more than I can endure. And you'd have to admit you could care less. You are like all the rest of them. If I died, they would send some flowers, hire another editor to take my place, and forget that I ever existed. It's a terrible thing to live with the thought that no one would really mourn when you are gone."

She was right. It is a terrible thing to live a life so isolated and unrelated to anyone that there would be no one to mourn when you are gone. Mourning is a sign of caring. Seen in that light, mourning is part of life's privileged relationship. It is the evidence of concern and love. The emptiness that comes when love is gone, or has never arrived, may well be the ultimate of loneliness.

We often think of the hermit as a lonely person. Back in the hills, the hermit, as we have traditionally thought of him, is alone and separated from all the rest of mankind. But whatever the injury or reason that led him to turn his back on civilization, we can be sure that he exercised his freedom in choosing to do so. But the hermits who live in the midst of our cities in quiet refinement and bleak desperation have not asked for their sad fate. They are a by-product of the disorganization of life that comes with rapid change and urban complexity. Their unwanted isolation and loneliness is probably a more severe threat to life than the chosen retreat from the community of men that sent the hermit to the hills.

Some hermits are not separated from people physically, but they cannot relate to them emotionally. We might call them psychological hermits. In a ward at a mental hospital I watched isolated people sitting in groups and staring blankly into space. They saw nothing. They did not pay attention to anything that went on around them. Their inner world was shut off from the world of communication, relationship, and activity.

Most people would not experience this form of mental and emotional separation from others, but all of us know at least to some minimal degree what it is like to be blocked from communication and relationship. We have a headache and do not want to talk. We may be injured in spirit and want to be left alone. We may be filled with shame and not want anyone to intrude on our painful self-awareness. Loneliness may have many causes, and it may show itself in many ways. Even those who may seem to be the center of the party in their boisterous participation may be covering up a feeling of separation and emptiness that plagues their lives.

But perhaps the most painful form of loneliness that can be experienced by a human is that which comes with the death of one who has been so dearly loved and been so close to the center of life that it seems life will never be the same without him. What about this loneliness?

The loneliness that accompanies acute grief is an assault on the meaning of life itself. It is a threat to the inner security system of an individual. It is a devastating loss of some of the essential nature of the self.

When a person loves another, he becomes vulnerable. When he is so concerned about another that whatever happens to them also happens to him, he extends the perimeters of his capacity to suffer. When a loved person is happy, the happiness is shared. So also when a loved person is injured, you can feel the injury. When a loved person is devastated by death, you feel the impact of great emotion. Part of that damage to life is caused by the fact that the part of yourself you invested in another has been temporarily lost. So the grief that is felt is a deep type of loneliness; the bereaved person is longing for the part of himself that he gave in love to another.

While the person who has died cannot be retrieved, and while that loss is final, we must ask, Is there something that can be done about the part of the self that was invested in the life of the dead person? Is this loneliness of one part of the self for its missing part something that can be resolved? If so, how?

In the slowly and painfully acquired wisdom of the race, men have learned to give some positive answers to these questions. But we have also learned from experience that men do not have to accept the positive answers. Strong emotion may pervert wisdom. There may be an inclination to reject the healthful answers, because the injury to the security system of the individual is so great that his impulse toward restored balance is paralyzed. He may get a perverse satisfaction out of wallowing in his loss and separation. He may misinterpret his feelings in such a way that he glories in his grief and tries to hold on to it as a proof of his love and willingness to suffer as a result of it.

These negative responses to loss may well cripple life and reduce it to a partial existence. The imposition of self-injury and extended grief upon life may satisfy some need for self-punishment, but it does nothing to free life for its fullest realization. While unhealthy grieving is not a rare phenomenon, it is never a life-fulfilling experience.

The loneliness that is so important a part of the complex emotion of grief must be appreciated for what it is if it is to be managed wisely. It is evidence of the empty spot in life that has been left by someone's death. It is a verification of the importance of that other person to life. It is a response of life to the loss of the object of love. It is a diminishing of the experience of life because the life that was shared can no longer be shared in the same way.

When we recognize the loneliness and the emptiness for what it is, we relieve some of the distress and misgiving we may have about it. It is nothing to fear or be ashamed of. It is a fact of life that verifies the fact of love. But as our life does not end with the death of another, so our capacity to love does not end with the loss of the object of our love. The capacity for love remains waiting for a chance to express itself anew in ways that can continue to enrich life.

There may be times, at first, when our love seems to be impacted by the feeling that any expression of it would be an act of disloyalty to the one we "have loved and lost a while." But a simple examination of that idea can quickly discount it. Love is not a static thing. It is not something that can be kept in limbo. If it has no object, it does not exist. In order to keep it alive, it must be brought into focus and directed toward some person. Love is not an event that happens or does not happen. It is a process that, like breathing, is bound up with life, and life remains fruitful when the process is active. To deny the process of love because the object of love is dead is to pass a death sentence upon one's self. This produces the hostile, resentful, sour personalities that deny the right of love to exist and then become prey to its opposite—hostility and hatred.

There may be times when the feeling of injury and the pain of loneliness are so great that a person feels something important within him has died. To the extent that he has experienced a life-enriching relationship, this appears to be true. But the object of the relationship is not the same thing as the capacity for relationship. Rather, it is one of the strongest verifications of that capacity. The task of the person experiencing the loneliness of bereavement is to verify his capacity for love by once again engaging in the process of expressing his love where it can bear fruit in creative living.

One of the more active parts of the support process that takes place at the time of death is the verification of the number of other relationships that exist in life and that can be expressions of the love one feels and needs. The coming together of family, friends, and community is a statement of sustaining love that is ongoing even though one love-object has died. Those who watch what takes place at a funeral are constantly made aware of the fact that what is important is not so much what is said at such times as what is implied by the coming together. In effect, the funeral verifies the many relationships that continue to be active in life, and the verification, in turn, gives meaning to the coming together.

The variety of ceremonial opportunities that are employed tend to enrich the various ways by which this supportive nature of the other loves of life can be amplified. The formal and informal, the close and the near close, the ceremonial and the personal—all communicate in their own way the importance of the relationships that express love and concern. The more ceremony, rite, and ritual, and the more opportunity for expression of feelings of love and concern, the more quickly and adequately can the verification of continued love in life occur.

When persons—through some false sense of pride or privacy—seek to separate themselves from this loving community, the more quickly and completely do they sentence themselves to painful and destructive expressions of their loneliness. In fact, by resisting those who love them and would seek to sustain them by their tender love and care, they tend to verify and confirm their separation from the world.

By accepting love and being willing to be the object of genuine concern, a bereaved person adds something to his own life and at the same time verifies an important process in the lives of others. He learns that even devastating circumstances can open doors to new meaning and new love. He experiences the awareness of continued growth and creativity, for he becomes aware of the fact that even the worst of life may reveal the best of life if he works to make it so. And loneliness may be enriching as well as distressing if managed properly.

Usually the loneliness that accompanies grief is so painful that we are not apt to spend much time thinking of how it might be used for the growth and enrichment of life. Perhaps it would be important for us now to think a bit about the creative uses of loneliness.

Perhaps the first thing we have to do is to shift gears from our preoccupation with the painful emotions that go with loneliness to the awareness of the positive possibilities that can come with being alone.

There is a difference between being lonely and being alone. Loneliness is an emotional state that may be quite painful, while being alone is a state of separation from others that can open doors to self-awareness and personal growth.

We have faced the painful possibilities of loneliness. Let us now look at the important opportunities that come with being alone. It is no mystery that we can often do things when we are alone that we would find it difficult to do when others are around. We can do the reading that we have often put off. We can listen to music that we like but is not popular with others. We can write the letters that have been neglected too long. We can do many things to use our alone-time well.

Henry David Thoreau fell deeply in love with Ellen Sewell, but was prevented from marrying her because her father did not approve of Thoreau's unusual ideas. So Thoreau nursed his lonely heart by taking long walks in the woods and developing another dimension of communication with nature. In a few years he built himself a little cabin on the shore of Walden Pond, outside of Concord, and went there to live. As he put it, he wanted to find the true meaning of his existence and to "suck the marrow out of life." In this experience of being deeply alone he made discoveries in himself, in nature, and in philosophy that combined to produce one of the great classics of American literature. He used his loneliness to discover the rich possibilities for growth in his aloneness.

When Admiral Byrd went off to a remote weather station in the Antarctic wastelands, it was because he felt it was too hazardous an assignment to give to anyone else. For months he went about the quiet tasks of his assignment—hundreds of miles from any other human. Not only did he study the winter climate and the weather variations where no one had spent a winter before, but he thought deep thoughts and experienced strange feelings that he recorded in a book he called simply "Alone." He found a way of giving creative expression to his aloneness.

Thomas Merton became a Trappist monk in order to discover the spiritual depths of his own being in quietness and meditation. Through years of self-discipline, he plumbed the deep recesses of his own being and shared it with others through his writings. One of his last little books was called *Thoughts on Solitude*. Herein he shows how solitude can add richness to the relationship between creature and Creator.

These three men—in quite different environments and circumstances—found that being alone gave them great opportunities for personal growth and creativity in living.

In our rather frantic whirl of activities, we lack the center of quietness from which calm and wise judgments can emerge. Writing in a business journal, a British industrialist recommended two periods of complete aloneness each day. For a half hour in the morning and afternoon he suggests receiving no phone calls, scheduling no appointments, and allowing no interruptions. During this time, one should sit quietly and think about oneself, one's responsibilities, and one's ways of being creative in meeting the challenges of life. The industrialist said that in his own quiet times things came into focus, and he gained the kind of perspective that could not grow from total busyness.

During recent years, I have spent many weeks with business and professional persons in what are called retreats or spiritual-life seminars. Almost always these sessions are held in quiet, remote, and rural settings. People may take long walks in the woods and hills or along the shores of lakes. Sometimes they sit together for long periods of time in front of a roaring fire. At other times, they talk about the things that, in other settings, are not easily mentioned. Sometimes these people report that they live more in the shared periods of retreat than they do in all the rest of their life-activity.

Across our country, thousands of small groups of people gather for an hour or two once a week to share their deep thoughts and feelings, often in long periods of complete silence. Here again they report times of self-discovery and insight that enrich all the rest of living.

For centuries, people have wondered what is the central component of what we all worship. They come together week after week to do quite the same things. On the surface, it may seem to be quite a futile and meaningless use of time. But perhaps something of great importance for life has been taking place; for at the same time that people seek to be alone with their own deepest thoughts and feelings, they receive the *support* of the group, and all share sympathetically in a common quest. Being alone together seems contradictory, but it may be one of life's essential activities. It may be that this is where people find worth for their own beings and inspiration to live their own lives creatively rather than in futile and unending desperation. Even the funeral is a time of being alone together. In paying tribute to a life that has been lived, it offers respect and appreciation for all life.

The sudden experience of painful loss and loneliness in life may be ameliorated if, through the quiet experience of love and useful self-discipline, we can learn to value our aloneness. If we can grow to feel comfortable with ourselves in such times of purposeful separation and quietness, we may be able to develop resources that can be of great use to us when the demands of life force us back upon ourselves.

We know that life becomes what it is through language, culture, and social relationship; and we would not dispense with that in any way. Rather, we would recommend times of alternation, when the meaning of the group life can be assimilated and evaluated in quiet times by ourselves alone. As with most things in life, we are impoverished if we reduce our choices to the either-or. Rather, we should discover the "both-ands" of life, through which we can have the experience of social as well as personal development. Then we can become so comfortable with ourselves that we never need fear being alone. We can cherish its possibilities. Then when life-circumstances compel us to adjust to a painful separation and the loneliness that is part of it, we will be prepared to use our aloneness for continued creative growth in living.

4

Grief and Humor

On the face of it, it would seem that grief and humor are at opposite poles of human emotion. Usually we agree that there is nothing funny about the painful emotion of deep grief. Yet we often observe seemingly inappropriate behavior among grieving persons, and humor, in particular, often surfaces where it would seem to be most out of place. Why so?

Psychologists tell us that fear of death is one of the basic human emotions. From early childhood, it is drilled into us that we must be careful or we might get killed. Children are cautioned to look both ways before crossing a street or they might be hit by a car. When the primal urge to climb a tree is acted upon, parents may stand at the foot of the tree and plead with the child to come down so that he won't fall and kill himself. All sorts of hazards to life are represented in their most powerful form as possible causes of death. It is not strange, with all of this conditioning early in life, that fear of death comes to be one of our most powerful emotions.

But when fear is omnipresent and perhaps lurking in unsuspected places, it is not strange for it to change into that diffuse fear we call anxiety. In fact, some philosophers, like Tillich, say that death-anxiety is the basic human emotion. It underlies our other fears and apprehensions about the process of living.

When we deal with such an all-pervading and unfocused emotion, it is not surprising that our anxiety leads to forms of acting out that may seem incongruous, for we are operating in the area of the nonrational. Seen in this light, some of those things that at first seemed inappropriate may make sense.

When we try to cope with any anxiety-creating area of life, we have a strong inclination to reduce it in size to something we think we can handle. So we often laugh at what we fear and joke about the things that basically are not very funny.

Perhaps there is no time death is a more constant threat than under battle conditions, when a whole army of the so-called enemy is bent on destroying the life of individuals on the opposing side. The richness of humor under these conditions is well known. Bill Mauldin made it possible for soldiers in combat situations to laugh at themselves and their plight. This released some of the tension and made it possible for them to keep going.

Each of us in our own way is engaged in a fight for life. Though the conditions are not as extreme as in war, the nature of the combat is constant and needs to be relieved through occasional release of emotion and reduction of stress.

It is interesting to watch people when they are faced with stress, and to assess the meaning of humor as it is employed in this context. It is not strange that in stressful times the number of TV programs founded on humor tends to increase. It is a response to a generally recognized need of people under stress. Cartoons make light of social problems, and the caricatures of political figures make them look less powerful and more human. We then can laugh at them as we laugh at ourselves, and the magnitude of the problems they represent seems to be reduced.

The comedy programs on TV tend to focus on certain specific areas. One comedian makes fun of women and marriage. Another comic situation laughs at war and the human suffering it causes. Another makes fun of the plight of those who are prisoners of war. Still another derives its humor from the emotional problems that send people to the psychologist's office. Often the clergyman is cast in a humorous role because the ultimate problems of life's meaning that he represents are so serious they can't be confronted directly.

Often it seems that the more morbid the humor, the more response it draws. This is not strange, for it is difficult not to be too extreme about the sources of man's extreme forms of stress. So the humor about death tends to be not only morbid but moribund, and the funeral director is given lines like, "Deadliness is next to Godliness" or "My work is really just a put-down" or "I really dig my work."

The proponents of women's liberation are the focal points of much joking. Here the ancient role of women, with all of the psychological problems that have been connected with it, is faced with rapid change and the insecurity that comes when old ways of doing things are rapidly disrupted. The long line of theatrical comedies that play on this theme of the uncertain status of the liberated woman and the resultantly insecure man goes on year after year. Part of the function of this type of humor is that it places the adjustments that must be made in a context that mitigates their potential seriousness, while improving the morale that makes the adjustments possible.

In my book *For the Living,* I pointed out that the mysterious areas of life and the anxiety-creating events of life need humor as a psychic lubricant. The tension-creating circumstances of life may be denied because they are too difficult to confront. This leads to repression—with all of its hazards. But these circumstances can be approached so as to master them. This is certainly one of the functions of humor; it reduces life's problems to the extent that they can be approached—first in humor, then in seriousness.

It is not strange, then, that the more serious the human problem, the more likely it is to become a subject for humor. Grief and humor are often bound together because of the depth of the human problem and the desperate need to find some way of coping with it. The humor may well serve as a handle for the problem—a way of cutting it down to manageable size.

We have looked at why apparently inappropriate behavior

may be a quite valid way of coping with the strong emotions of grief. Now let us look at what humor actually does in the release of stress.

From the physical point of view, the cause-effect factors that are operative are quite clear. Anxiety tends to cause physical stress. When you are upset and anxious, you may be aware of tension developing in your muscle system. The increase of muscle tension causes unusual pulling on the skeletal frame (to which the muscles are attached), and this in turn causes pressure on major nerve centers such as the spinal cord. Thus it is not unusual for a person under stress to have backaches, headaches, or neckaches.

Muscle spasticity, as a response to anxiety, can cause various aches and pains all over the body. Therefore, anything that can reduce anxiety can also be expected to release muscle spasticity and thus tension and pain. When a person is worrying about himself, for example, he may have a generalized feeling of discomfort. If something happens to alter the focus of his attention, he may realize that the discomfort has been reduced. The diffused anxiety may have been replaced by a specific condition that claimed his attention and led to specific action. The unspecified cause of his anxiety would then tend to be reduced.

Humor serves a physical purpose in that it reduces the tension that leads to spasticity and pain. What is it that laughing does? It engages two muscle systems that can be the center of much tension—the lower jaw and the diaphragm. If you have ever watched someone under stress, you may have observed the powerful muscle just below the ear at the end of the jawbone expanding and contracting. This muscle action reflects tension.

If you have ever been distressed, you may have felt the buildup of tension in the large muscle system that separates the organs in the chest cage from the visceral organs below it. We have various ways of referring to this tension, but they all mean the same thing. We may say, "I have butterflies in my stomach," "Am I up tight," "It hit me in the pit of my stomach," or "My heart sank." All these common forms of speech refer to the muscular tension that gathers in the region of the diaphragm.

When there is a buildup of tension in this facial or abdominal region, there is a need for a form of release that can reduce the stress. This is essential to our health and healthful functioning. Laughing and crying are usually the most accessible forms of this release. Both produce a spontaneous shaking of the muscles involved in such a way that the spasticity is reduced. Actually, the muscle systems involved in laughing and crying are much the same. A "belly laugh" may do the same thing as a "belly cry."

The value of this humorous approach is illustrated by the public reaction to a book that appeared a decade or so ago. Jessica Mitford wrote a sardonically humorous book about the funeral as she observed it. For a long time, the subject had been taboo. The few serious works on the subject had been largely ignored. But now the light touch came along, and people began to laugh about death and funerals. The fact that the book was so obviously a caricature based on distorted emotion rather than research allowed the readers to get beyond the seriousness that had surrounded the subject and laugh a little.

The results have been most interesting. The serious recommendations of the book have largely been ignored. These were for more cremations and more memorial societies. The number of cremations percentagewise has been about the same for the last twenty years, and the growth of memorial societies has been spotty and minimal over the country at large. But the indirect effects of confronting death, even sardonically, has opened up a whole new field of study and research. Professional journals have been started for studies of death. Three hundred universities and colleges now offer death studies as a regular part of the curriculum, and over two thousand high schools offer courses in death perspectives. What serious studies seemed unable to accomplish, a humorous book could.

Even the funeral director has learned to laugh at himself. And if anyone needs a bit of humor, it is the man whose professional role obliges him to cope with the more gruesome and tragic aspects of community life. He must serve when accidents, murder, suicide, and wasting disease destroy life. So he should be able to laugh with his peers at the foibles of the clergy and the medical examiner. But underneath it all, he is exercising his right to cope with the anxieties he feels in the unusual role he performs in the community.

To the community, the funeral director is a permanent symbol of the inevitability of death. Part of his function is to confront the reality of death with the dignity and understanding that helps people face their anxiety with assurance. He well knows that there are times when the humor is thinly disguised anguish, and when the distorted makeup of the clown masks a heart that is breaking.

In our effort to understand the interrelation of grief and humor, it is important to realize that humor is an effort to manage feelings that are perhaps too great to cope with normally. It would be unfortunate if anyone were so lacking in his perception of humor's role that he would take such humor personally. It is seldom directed *at* a person, but rather *through* the person to the source of the anxiety—death, death's impact, and the common fear we harbor toward it.

Yes, grief and humor are related—but in a useful and valid way. So, though it seems out of place, it may well have a special place at special times and places; and we should understand and tolerate its manifestations because we understand its meaning and its purpose.

Perhaps someone, someday, will prepare an anthology of the types of humor that people use to confront their anxiety about death. It would probably show that although the humor appears to be directed at priests, ministers, funeral directors, and doctors, its real object is the fear of death, and the people toward whom it is directed are merely the agents for releasing the stress. In a sense, therefore, the object of the humor is also complimented by the humor; for he is usually a person who is respected and trusted to be understanding.

When we look closely at community practices and traditions, we realize that there are many ways that people try to manage their anxiety about death. Let us take a couple of examples.

Halloween is a time for parties and outlandish behavior. The theme, no matter how well disguised, is death. Some of the most acute anxiety about death is felt by parents. The death of a child always seems unjust and untimely—out of context with life's normal expectations. On Halloween, parents can act out this anxiety in a socially accepted pattern. They dress their children up in the symbols of death—skeleton suits, death masks, and ghostly attire. They send their children out into the night, aware of the hazards, but willing to live with them on a temporary basis so as to have it all over with and back to normal in a few hours.

If a person were to stand back and take an objective view of the strange and bizarre behavior that takes place on this one evening, he would have difficulty making sense of it—unless he sensed its deeper meaning. For the acceptance of Halloween by parents probably expresses their need for a symbolic, socially approved way of coping with their particular form of death-anxiety.

The intensity with which Halloween is prepared for, commercialized, and socially approved may be a clue to the degree of death-anxiety parents feel in our culture. The structure of the nuclear family, with its limitation of offspring, tends to increase the emotional investment made in each individual child and thus to make this form of emotional release all the more necessary.

While some of our symbolic behavior is lighthearted and humorous, some also is somber and intensely religious. The holy drama of the death and resurrection of Jesus of Nazareth is the high point of the calendar. While it is lacking in humor, its function may well be related to the emotional needs expressed in the sportive counterpart that occurs between one Easter season and the next—Halloween.

When we confront death honestly, whether in jest or seriousness, we may well reduce the intense anxiety that surrounds the emotional hazard.

Cultural patterns may determine whether the form of release employed is laughing or crying. In some places crying is expected and approved. In other places crying is inter-preted as a sign of weakness, so the more acceptable form of release would involve laughter.

Either way, it is quite clear that a valid physical function is served by the use of these methods of relaxing muscle tension. They are useful. They are good.

But there are psychological as well as physical needs triggered by grief. It not only generates muscle tension but nervous tension as well. The latter, too, needs to have some form of release.

Our nervous tensions tend to develop when there is a problem so great that we cannot cope with it through the conventional techniques of problem solving. The unusual events of life may call for unusual coping devices. Humor is often employed as such a coping device.

When we can laugh at something, we tend to reduce its magnitude as a threat. Sex in the civilized framework within which we live tends to cause stress and anxiety. When we can laugh about sex and make fun of sex, then it is not so apt to make fools of us. So we tell jokes that are centered about childish concepts of sex, and all at once the whole idea fits into a simpler context and seems more manageable.

The social problems that cause emotional problems are often so overwhelming that we see no way of solving them. But once we laugh about them, they seem less threatening. At least temporarily, our anxiety is reduced. Bill Crosby makes us laugh at our racial foibles just as Jack Benny helped us laugh at poverty and its penurious side effects.

A recent study shows that insomnia may be caused by an unconscious fear of death. A person may not know that he equates sleep with death, but his organic behavior may act it out. With the aged, Dr. Herman Feifel finds that a major hazard is unconscious fear of death. Relentlessly, old people approach the end of life. But they can be slowed down a bit by being able to laugh at their infirmities. So we have the "aging" jokes—about the hills that weren't there before or the physical activities that are now limited. An old man says: "I still like to look at pretty girls, but I can't remember why" or "It looks as if I'm going to have to have an operation on my prostitute gland."

Physically, psychologically, and socially, therefore, the humor we employ to face grief may be a useful and necessary device for reducing our anxieties to manageable size. What may seem inappropriate is, in context, quite valid indeed.

5

Grief and Self-Deceit

One does not live long without learning that threats to life become the sources of seriously modified behavior. When life is threatened, we often see the evidence of nonrational actions. People who usually act in competent and responsible ways may become erratic and uncertain when they are subjected to the stress and pressure of assaults on their security or their established ways of life.

Anatomically, we know that life-threatening circumstances trigger a release of defense mechanisms. Often these mechanisms are so completely automatic that there is no chance for them to be lifted up to rational examination.

If someone steps on your toe, there is no long period of decision-making involved in your response. You instantly jerk your foot out from under the painful weight. Similarly, if you are caught in a circumstance that threatens your integrity as a person, your first impulse is to react in a way that is protective of that integrity. For many, the first impulse may be to engage in some form of deceit.

This form of deceit is certainly not new. In some of our oldest literature, it comes through loud and clear. In the legend of the Garden of Eden, when Adam is discovered eating the forbidden fruit, he says, in effect, "It wasn't my fault. Eve made me do it."

When the whole sorry mess of Watergate began to collapse

around the heads of those who were its perpetrators, the self-defensive process we observed included blaming others, calling others liars, covering up earlier falsehoods, and seeking to assign high motives to low behavior. The conspirators wanted to convince themselves that they had acted in the best interests of the country.

Whenever any form of self-deceit is engaged in, it becomes quickly evident that people lose their sense of perspective and their grasp on reality. As a result, it becomes increasingly difficult for them to function wisely in the circumstances that surround them.

What we observe in other contexts is certainly true of the person who is confronted by a life-threatening event that overtaxes his resources for wise management of the crisis. Grief can be this form of devastating event, and defense against it may take the form of self-deceit.

We will explore this type of response in the context of three separate categories, even though it is quite obvious that the categories are interrelated and difficult to isolate. However, it may help us—by bringing some of the problems into focus—to look at three different ways in which self-deceit can distort reality. For sometimes we try to change physical reality itself; sometimes we try to use reason to confound the reasonable; and sometimes we try to find a cosmic dimension for our distress and thereby project our self-deceit out upon the universe.

Our body systems are designed to work best in a world of reality. Use of a polygraph, or lie detector, is feasible only because body systems usually function normally under conditions of telling the truth, and become erratic when deceit is used. Blood pressure, skin texture, digestive processes, and respiration show deviation on the graphs as soon as truth is violated.

Because we have a natural abhorrence of falsehood, we are apt to engage in more subtle forms of deceit, and so make it more difficult to confront the meaning of our own behavior. We seldom ever lie boldly, thinking to ourselves, "That is a lie." Rather, we use subtle devices that tend to outwit our moral censors and bypass our sensitivity of conscience. We use self-justification as if it were free of self-deceit. We blame others without realizing that it is a deceitful distortion of the way things really are.

When acute grief confronts us, it is important to examine our possible forms of self-deception in order to begin to cope with our emotions more honestly.

When the impact of acute grief is experienced, it is often our strong impulse to blame the doctor, the nurse, the police officer, or the funeral director. Bereaved persons often try to justify their efforts at self-deception by bringing malpractice suits against physicians. And many are the nurses who have borne the full assault of hostile and accusing words from the newly bereft.

While blaming others tends to deny reality, even more direct forms of denial are often observed. People will assume that if they deny the fact of death, they will be relieved of the pains of their grief. Thus they may seek the immediate removal of the evidence of death. They may seek quick cremation and deny themselves the chance to act out their feelings in recognized ceremonial form. This type of self-deceit may have serious aftereffects as the real feelings seek to find delayed expression. When normal expression is denied, the sad result may be unhealthful detours that lead to illness and personality change.

Often those who are intellectually adept and highly skilled in rational processes most easily resort to forms of self-deception. Their facility with ideas may cover up a lack of competence in handling their feelings. That is probably why most of the unhealthy modes of self-deception in facing the reality of death and grief come from university communities. The dependence on rationalizations to escape the impact of feelings may lead to emotional problems that are actually more difficult to manage.

Self-deception may work itself into the funeral process so that people distort the purpose of healthful acting-out and use the funeral to support their rationalizations. Pastors tend to spiritualize death. Physicians tend to sedate the grieving. Funeral directors tend to generalize death. All are ways of escaping the unique demands of the emotions in a given circumstance. All are efforts to avoid responsibility to one's own emotions and to the deep feelings of others.

Blaming others, on the one hand, may be balanced by an unreasonable effort to blame oneself for circumstances over which one has had little control. Denial of responsibility when it does exist, however, may be equally reality-distorting. And escape from healthful modes of emotional expression may be quite as damaging to the total person as any other form of unwise crisis management. To reject your own inner feelings is a denial of an important part of the self.

In the interest of health, it is essential for the grief-stricken individual to make a valiant effort to move beyond self-deceit and boldly confront the reality that exists. If he is to become a whole person once again, he needs to abandon his grief for a new and creative phase of living.

The form of self-deceit that tries to confound the rational is often observed in times of emotional crisis. Those who appear to be most vulnerable to this form of distorted perception are those who have developed special skills in using their intellectual ability. People who approach each life-situation with a logical and rational stance begin to depend on their mental abilities to cope with life. While in many situations, this is a valuable resource, there are times when it may become hazardous.

Emotions have their own integrity. They must be accepted as real and valid parts of life. To try to suppress or divert the energy of emotions through purely rational processes can throw life out of balance. Reason is essential where reasonable approaches are valid. Reason may be employed as an escape from reality when powerful emotions are involved.

Some forms of mental illness are the result of perversions of the thinking processes. At a deep and perhaps unconsious level a person may deceive himself so completely about his relations to other people and the universe that he tends to become nonfunctional. His distortions become so great that they blot out his capacity to see things as they are.

For instance, the paranoid person may become so suspicious of others that he thinks they are enemies out to destroy his life. He may starve himself because he thinks people are trying to poison his food. He may avoid proper medical care because he is suspicious of doctors and thinks they are trying to kill him. He may turn against his family and friends because he feels they cannot be trusted. A reasonable sense of caution that is valuable for life is blown out of proportion to the realities of life. The self-deception implicit in paranoia may make it impossible for a person to live a normal life.

The schizoid person fractures reality in another way. He becomes so distressed in his efforts to cope with the real world that he finally gives up. He withdraws from the world he should be encountering, and builds for himself an unreal world in which he can deny his problems and the stresses that go with them. However, this make-believe world is a basic deceit; for there is no such world except in the anguished imagination of the person who creates it. That person does not recover until he finds the way back to the real world and develops resources for coping with it adequately.

So it is that the depressed person distorts reality in another way. He deceives himself into thinking that all is hopeless. He exaggerates his distresses, and reduces his abilities and resources. All in all, he creates a deceptive picture of his life and his world. Then he has great difficulty in working within this distorted perception of reality. He is not apt to find a way out of his illness until he is able to end his self-deceit and see himself and his world more honestly. Although the motivation for his distortions of reality may be buried deep in his lower levels of consciousness, he cannot function well until he is able to substitute more honest motivations for the abnormal drives that have made his life a shambles.

What we see in the more extreme forms of self-deceit, in which a person drives himself to severe life-disrupting behavior, may also be manifested in milder forms among people who have trouble coping with the routine emotional crises of their lives.

When death comes in tragic and untimely fashion, the overwhelming impact of the experience may be more than the emotions can handle, so the coping tasks may be taken over by the rationalizing and denying processes of intellectualization.

A sophisticated woman who prided herself on her firm grip on emotions and her skill in managing crises decided, when her husband died suddenly of a heart attack, to have no service, no notice in the paper, no visitation. She said to herself, "Let's face it. He's dead. I can't change a thing of the past. Get rid of the body as fast as I can, for it's no good to anyone now. Then I can go on living with my good common sense, for the future is the only thing I can do anything about anyway." Listened to as she put it, it sounded brave and sensible. But the basic error in her approach to her husband's death was that she lied to herself about her own deep feelings. Through years of association, her husband's body had become important to her. She needed some way of disposing of it that was compatible with her feelings about it. She needed ceremonial activity that gave her a chance to act out the feelings that were too deep to be expressed in words or easy intellectualizations.

Six months after her husband's death she was on the verge of nervous collapse. She called a counselor and asked, "When is this dreadful nightmare ever going to end? Every day I get letters and phone calls from people who have just heard of my husband's death. This whole thing is drawn out endlessly, and I can't take it any longer." Her basic efforts at self-deception projected themselves outward until they were compounded many times over. Her counselor had to take her back in time to confront her own feelings, deal with them realistically, and then prepare for facing the future with complete honesty.

Dr. William M. Lamers, Jr., a West Coast psychiatrist, defines a funeral as "an organized, purposeful, time-limited, flexible, group-centered response to death." It has implicit within its process an honesty in confronting a painful reality of life. To escape from this honest confrontation, no matter how sophisticated a person tries to be about it, tends to be a form of self-deception that can only complicate the problems of coming to terms with life. Intellectualizations may sound good, but they may be convenient forms of lying that in the long run make the truth more difficult to live with.

Sometimes our fantasies involve other persons. A childhood fantasy may make a child feel close to a hero. The image of the hero may be a stimulus to achieve proficiency in sports or in the arts. But when persons are so engrossed in their fantasies of being someone else that they lose sight of who they really are, the problems begin to emerge. The self that deceives itself into being another self has lost touch with reality.

Similarly, the person who imagines unreal things about the motives and goals of another person may distort his life-picture. Jealousy is born of the unhealthy self-deceit that invariably accompanies insecurity and uncertainty. Many a person has made himself miserable by attributing to another his own hostilities and prejudices. A man with a good education and fine position resented the fact that a neighbor had inherited some wealth and had attended an Ivy League university. He was always measuring himself by what the other man owned, said, and did. He finally began to feel so insecure that he accused his wife of falling in love with the neighbor. Out of his compounded self-deceptions he created an atmosphere that threatened his own best interests. It was not an easy task to talk him out of his major self-deceptions.

The many forms of self-deception that exist in life may come together at the very point that the major stress and anguish of grief are experienced. A person may want to deny the reality of death itself, but that does no good; for sooner or later a person must begin to live with a world that has changed. A person may want to accuse and punish himself for things that he has not done—as if by some magic the self-punishment could make things right again. Or he may develop unhealthy resentments and hostilities against others—as if they were to blame for the tragic circumstances that have engulfed him.

Dr. Erich Lindemann, a wise and trusted authority on the management of acute grief, says that the basic requirement for working through the problems of grief is to deal with reality as fully and as quickly as possible. There is no therapy in creating a world of falsehoods or dishonest denials. As quickly as a person can marshal his resources, he should honestly face the pain of his deep feelings and express them with openness and sincerity. As soon as is reasonable, he should be open and responsive to the feelings of others; for many persons share his bereavement. And as soon as it is possible, he should confront the tasks of reordering his life to assess its needs and the resources available to meet the needs.

Perhaps one of the deepest needs of those who confront the distress of acute grief is to be kind to themselves. And it is certainly not being kind to oneself to entangle one's life in a mass of fantasies and vehicles of self-deception. Nor is it useful to assume one is so strong that one never needs help; for there are times in life when all of us can benefit from the strength, guidance, and wisdom of others whose perspective has not been clouded by the stress of acute grief.

Self-deceit may reveal itself in many ways. It may be blunt or subtle, immediate or delayed, open or disguised. But, however it shows itself—and it is bound to make its appearance during the times of acute stress—try to see it for what it is and avoid the added difficulty that it can cause at a time when there is trouble enough.

Perhaps one of the most common forms of self-deceit is engaged in unconsciously. It is the tendency of people under stress to live with fantasies and delusions rather than with the reality that is essential to the healthful resolution of their problems.

Sometimes these fantasies have a cosmic dimension. A person may dredge up some neurotic guilt and attach it to a tragic circumstance, thereby becoming convinced that God is using the painful event to punish him for his misdeed. If we think of the universe as controlled by cosmic law and order, it is hard to make room for this type of capricious deity; nevertheless, it is quite common to hear people gasp, "Oh, why did God do this to me?" Such attitudes, though easily understood, distort the basic structure of the universe in a way that may make a person doubly vulnerable to the crises of life.

Once a person begins to fantasize, he is apt to create other and less valid fantasies to support his previous ones. He may look to soothsayers for understanding, overlooking those who could fortify his sense of what is real and valid. And, at the same time, he may turn against a potential source of satisfying his emotional needs because of his exaggerated feelings of guilt. Then at a time when a friendly cosmic force is most needed, God may become an enemy rather than a friend.

Some fantasies specialize in magic. They assume (1) that there are weaknesses in the universal structure of law and order and (2) that if a person seeks diligently he may be able to find these weakness and take advantage of his special knowledge. Miracles and magic may not be far apart. Many religious traditions have built upon this impulse to fantasize in times of stress. When people are promised the miraculous or the magical, this support for their fantasy system encourages them to move further away from their trust in a basic law and order at work in all of creation.

The self-deceiving uses of fantasy may start with one's self. In fact, a person may use something that is not true in order to support a true need. Early in life, for instance, he may have discovered that the days he was ill were special days. He received more love and concern than usual. Sometimes he was given presents and special foods. People hovered about him with concerned looks on their faces, and he would be free from punishment. Not only was he liberated from homework and school chores, but he was excused from much of the unpleasantness of life. He was not scolded, and was allowed to do what he wanted to do within the bounds of his sickroom.

Years later, the stresses and pressures begin to build up, and the burdens of life seem intolerable. Deep down inside of him something says, "If you get sick, everything will be all right." So he deceives himself into feeling ill, and before long he finds himself in bed, with tender love and care, more concern, and freedom from the many tasks that had been producing the stresses in his life. It takes an honest and perceptive person to employ the clear sense of reality to avoid such a trap of self-deception. While at times there may be some value in healthful and useful fantasies, there is a greater danger that they will be used to undermine the healthful confrontation of life and its problems.

6

Grief and Depression

One of the more distressing emotional states one can experience is depression. It is as if a heavy weight has been placed upon life. Everything seems more difficult to do, and the burdens of life seem intolerable. Each day dawns as if it is to be another time of trial; evening comes with the prospect of troubled sleep.

In our day, depression is perhaps the most common form of emotional distress. It is the most apt to interfere with the creative work of college students, and it has its special impact on those who in middle years feel let down, frustrated, and faced with subtle forms of failure. It can be an active ingredient in the distresses of old age, when life seems to be running out, gainful employment is past, and the specter of death looms unrelenting somewhere in the future.

For the counselor, it is quite obvious that the largest percentage of those who seek special help will be faced with what is called the depressive syndrome. And often it is difficult to communicate with and relate to the depressed person, simply because the person feels that nothing matters and that even his discomfort must be tolerated because there is no way out of his painful state of consciousness.

In order to approach this distressing state with some possibility of ameliorating its painfulness, we need to make some distinctions and sharpen up our definitions. From the earliest records of man come descriptions of depression and its behavioral consequences. Young David played his harp because the sweet music relieved the depression of King Saul. The early word that was often used to describe depression was *melancholia,* or "the state of being melancholy." The ancient drama of Job seems to be an in-depth examination of depression and the methods that might be employed to fight one's way out of the complex and painful feelings that characterize it.

The National Association for Mental Health gives a broad, working definition as follows: "Depression is an emotional state of dejection and sadness, ranging from mild discouragement and down-heartedness to feelings of utter hopelessness and despair."

With that as a starting point, we need to move on to some distinctions as to types and severity of the emotional distress. First, we recognize that there are types of depression that can be called situational or reactive, because the cause-effect factors are clearly evident. In an athletic event, the winner feels elated, while the person who tried just as hard but lost feels let down, dejected, and depressed. Here the reason is obvious; the effect is clearly related to the cause, and we all feel that quite soon the person will have resolved his distress and be ready to try again.

Second, we recognize that there are depressive states in which the cause-effect relationship is not apparent. Here a person seems to be struggling with some inner process in which cause and effect seem unrelated or at least obscure. This form of depression tends to be more difficult to manage because the causes may be related to body chemistry, to deep threats to the value system of the individual, or to an accumulation of life-circumstances that produce an intolerable stress. This inner condition may produce forms of instability that cause the patient to move from deep depression to false elation. Thus false elation is but another phase of the depressive state.

For our own purposes, we will avoid the more distressing forms of the depressive state and try to limit our discussion to the type of depression that is apt to manifest itself at the time of acute grief and bereavement. But we would make it clear that this effort to limit the area of discussion should not be misconstrued as assuming that acute grief produces only the more manageable types of depression. When the conditions within the personality are propitious, the event of bereavement may precipitate the inner loss of balance that could produce clinical, psychotic, or severe depression. But this extreme manifestation would be far less common than the emotional state we would classify as reactive, where the cause-effect process produces the symptoms, and the normal resources of the person and society tend to restore balance so that the person can move out of depression and back into normal functioning.

From this point in our exploration of depression, we will be staying close to the research and phenomena that are most commonly observed in the reaction of persons to the loss, through death, of an important person in their life-pattern. The term most often employed to describe the varied physical, psychological, emotional, and behavioral manifestations is to say that the person is "in grief."

Grief is a normal neurosis. And, like a number of painful life-situations, it may produce temporary difficulties in functioning. Human relations may become complicated. A person may say and do things that are out of character. The thoughts and feelings during such a temporary period may be marked by a tendency to revert to earlier forms of problem-solving.

Normal neuroses may be observed in adolescence, involution, climacteric, or senescence. Here they are usually related to change in glandular function and the impact of changes in body chemistry upon attitudes and behavior. Sometimes it shows up in times of acute stress, such as accidents, when for a short while the person is in shock and nonfunctional. When a boxer is knocked out, he is temporarily nonfunctional, and the cause-effect process is clearly explainable. Temporary but normal neurotic states might be comparable; for emotional impact does things to a person, and temporary changes in behavior and personality may be observed.

Grief as a normal neurosis with depressive manifestations

is, on a temporary basis, not an uncommon response to acute loss. Its characteristics are usually feelings of low self-esteem, helplessness, and hopelessness. Let us examine these emotional states more in depth.

Loss of self-esteem can be a painful feeling. If we cannot love ourselves, how can we expect to be worthy of the love of others? If we harbor feelings of self-hatred, how can we marshal the energies of life for creative action?

Why would anyone experience feelings of low self-esteem? While we may not usually believe it, we are apt to be our own most severe critics. When our self-criticism is carried to an extreme, we can even become our own worst enemies. If you stop to listen to some of the things you say to yourself during a period of depression, you might be amazed. We blurt out self-judgments that are so vicious and cruel that we would probably be deeply offended if anyone else said such things about us.

Whenever we face acute grief, there are apt to be deep feelings of guilt. As we mentioned in an earlier chapter, this guilt may be difficult to manage; for it can show itself in obscured and varied form. But when this feeling is turned in against the self, it can produce the mood of depression. It may never be formalized in words, but the feelings themselves are strong enough to have the effect on the inner being of condemnation and judgment. This quite naturally leads to the mood of depression that is a by-product of the loss of self-esteem.

When you find it difficult to be comfortable with yourself—your own inner being—you have a real problem, for you cannot get away from yourself. You may try. You may watch soap operas, read escapist books, or throw yourself into frenetic recreation or trivial pastimes. But whenever there is a lull in activity, there you are again—with the same feelings and the same judgments. The escape from low self-esteem does not come through trying to outwit the self. Rather, it comes with a resolution of the inner conflict—by making peace within. This may be the result of as simple a process as talking to yourself.

You may say, "I did the best I knew how at the time." "I

know I am not perfect; but, given the circumstances, I did as well as anyone could." Through comparable efforts, it may be possible for the conscious mind to feed the lower levels of consciousness with the feelings that can give it inner comfort and cause it to modify its self-judgments.

When it seems impossible for this form of communication within the self to take place, the next step may be to use the resources of a skilled counselor or understanding friend to help you face the reality of your situation. Rather than support your cruel self-judgments, the other person could help you clarify relationships and conceptualize a more accurate balance sheet for your deep feelings. Sometimes just the passage of time will slowly but surely bring an inner balance to self-esteem, replacing self-judgment with a more objective perspective.

There are times, however, when life is faced with an irreversible process, and there occurs an overwhelming sense of helplessness. Most of the time in life we feel that we have some control over circumstances. We can do something about what is happening. But when death occurs, it is a confrontation with the inevitable. We cannot go back and change anything. This is such a different circumstance for most of us that we are apt to feel completely helpless in the face of unchangeable events.

When the feeling of helplessness is added to the loss of self-esteem, the person not only feels threatened by his inner attitude but also by outer circumstance. His feelings of personal incompetence are compounded by the conviction that even if he were competent, it would serve no purpose; for there would be no valid action that could be taken.

The helpless person is faced with the feeling that any purposeful action is impacted by things that are beyond his control, and that there is really nothing he can do about the cause of his distress. This leads to a more painful state of dejection, a loss of interest in life itself, a further restraint upon any purposeful action, and a threat to his affective capacity—his ability to direct his emotions into creative and loving relationships.

External circumstance that would normally lead to a

person's corrective action, therefore, produces a reversal of the basic condition of his life, and he reverts to inaction. In fact, he may be paralyzed. The restraint on muscular activity that is produced by this loss of motivation then aggravates the physical condition, for the inactivity progressively inhibits the functioning of the autonomic nervous system. The blood circulates more slowly, the poisons in the blood are not oxidized, and the system becomes sluggish. When this happens, the physical symptoms of the depressed state tend to increase, and the physical supplements the emotional in terms of the downward spiral of organic states.

The frustration that accompanies the feelings of helplessness produces the form of suppressed anger that is easily turned against the self to compound the state of depression. One of the more insidious aspects of the depressive state is that it feeds upon itself; that is, the state of being depressed tends to make a person feel even more depressed. The downward spiral of emotional distress may seem like a bottomless pit; for when the depressed person feels helpless to cope with outer circumstances, his inner state deteriorates also, and soon he feels incapable of any action at all. He is doubly helpless. It is little wonder, then, that the loss of self-esteem and the feelings of helplessness feed upon each other until the depressed person is ready to give up; for he is faced with intolerable odds—or at least that is the way it looks to him. Why try when it is obvious that effort can serve no purpose?

It quite naturally follows that low self-esteem compounded by the feelings of helplessness leads to the condition of hopelessness. If there is nothing that can be done to change the intolerable condition, what is the use of trying? There is nothing left but to give up and be swept along by the terrible state of affairs. The utter hopelessness of the depressive adds the final dimension to his sorry state of being.

The old Shakespearean adage "Hope springs eternal in the human breast" does not seem valid to the depressed person. In contrast, he is likely to be more at home with the sentiments of Alexander Pope—"Past hope, past cure, past help."

When this state of hopelessness is the result of acute grief, it is quite common for the bereaved person to be constantly preoccupied with the image of the dead person, dwelling on this mental activity so constantly that it deepens the feelings of helplessness to cope with life. This preoccupation tends to enhance a state of hypersensitivity to criticism, which in turn increases self-judgment, loss of self-esteem, and feelings of guilt.

Even in those situations in which death brings relief from long periods of pain, there is a feeling of guilt; for the surviving person tends to think it is a rejection of life to have welcomed the death of another. In the case of the person who is already moving toward a depressive state, this is a further nudge in the downward progression.

The depressed person tends to be irritable and sharp with those who show the most concern for his welfare. Because he knows he should not engage in this hostile behavior, he compounds his self-judgment by tending to become even more depressed by his own distressing behavior.

So the loss of self-esteem, compounded by helplessness and hopelessness, appears to create a state of being that is almost impossible to resolve. Yet we know that most persons who experience these emotional states in which cause-effect factors are clearly discernable, move through them and emerge as healthy, well-organized persons again. This being the case, what can we assume about inner restorative processes and forms of therapeutic intervention applicable to persons who are experiencing forms of situational depression?

First, we can assume that the forward momentum of life has within it the healing elements. If the depressive state does not become too overwhelming and the circumstances of life do not become unreasonably complicated, the chances are that the inner processes of the individual will eventually tend to produce a state of intropsychic balance.

Part of this is purely physiological. The excess glandular activity, with its modifications of body chemicals, will be gradually restored to balance as the chemicals are used up or neutralized. The hazards develop when the emotional state becomes chronic rather than transitory. Thus, time, in this respect, is a factor that moves a person away from trauma and toward health.

Second, there are some rather simple devices that can be used to modify the abnormal states of chemical imbalance. Karl Menninger suggests taking a long hike. This increases muscular activity, which in turn increases deep breathing, with better oxygenation of the blood. Also, the physical exertion stimulates visceral activity and uses up the excess chemicals secreted into the blood by glandular hyperactivity. This large-muscle activity tends to produce healthful forms of fatigue that in turn induce healthful sleep.

Third, there are forms of healthful acting-out that make it possible for body, mind, and spirit to be engaged simultaneously in activities that give creative direction to living. Rites, rituals, and ceremonies not only have their momentum, but they tend to move people along in healthful patterns of emotional expression. Anthropological studies point out that every culture has surrounded life crises with the forms of ceremony that keep life moving ahead, while at the same time providing opportunities for large-muscle activity, emotional expression, and group support. Perhaps this is why researchers are discovering that old-fashioned funerals, which afford an opportunity for a wide variety of acting out, are far more therapeutic than the minifunerals that some people, who are afraid of their deep feelings, are now substituting. The new trend toward reduction of the opportunity for acting out of deep feelings appears to be a denial of what is needed most at the very time it is needed most.

Fourth, there are community resources for counseling that make it possible for a person to talk out some of his more painful feelings. The professional counselor knows how painful a state of depression may be. The professional person accepts the painful feelings for what they are and helps the distressed person to examine and move beyond them. When a state of depression lasts more than a few days, it can be considered that the distressed person is entitled to the special forms of therapeutic intervention that can reduce the suffering and hasten recovery.

Almost everyone has weathered short periods of depression. So we are all aware of how distressing a state this can be. It is easy to imagine how disturbing it must be for a person to struggle against this emotional condition for an extended period of time. In many instances, outside intervention can relieve the stress by hastening the process of restoration.

Because acute grief often produces depressive reactions, it is important for the bereaved person to understand what is happening within him. It is important, also, for the professional involved to be especially alert to symptoms of unusual distress. Then he must take steps to help move the depressed person toward health and wholeness of being.

7

Grief and
Ceremonial Acting-out

Research in archaeology and anthropology in the last few years has thrown light on the meaning and value of rites, rituals, and ceremonies. It now becomes clear that our racial ancestors had acquired deep insight into their emotions and into the needs these emotions produced. With a spontaneous form of wisdom, they developed the processes that could meet these needs.

This has led us to a new and more meaningful exploration of the nature and significance of ceremonies of various sorts. It has made it possible for us to identify them as basic therapeutic resources for meeting the crises of life. In fact, most of the traditional ceremonies are centered around the potentially traumatic events or circumstances that are a part of normal living.

It seems that primitive man's deep respect for his feelings caused him to seek ways of venting them when the circumstances of life placed him under great stress. This folk wisdom seemed well on its way to being lost when psychologists and other personality researchers like Geoffrey Gorer, Rollo May, and Lawrence Abt began to study these rites, rituals, and ceremonies in depth and discovered that they may be the most valid and easily accessible resources available to man for working out his deep feelings. It may well be that the incidence of mental and emotional illness is proportionate to the loss of the resources available for ceremonial acting-out.

In his book *Future Shock*, Alvin Toffler has pointed out that the old ways of doing things embodied values that have too often been lost in the hurry and bustle of modern life. When an average family moves once every four years, it becomes quite obvious that many old ways of doing things will be pulled up by the roots along with the people.

Ethnic patterns of behavior that have been handed down from generation to generation have implicit in their structures a meaning that can be understood and acted upon by people who are in stress. Those who surround them can also appreciate the role they play in the acting-out process, and this makes it easy for them to enter into the therapeutic activity without even realizing what they are doing.

What have they discovered to be the nature of this healing process that is implicit in acting out? Students of rites, rituals, and ceremonies indicate that there are at least four common elements that are significant. There is meaning, message, group support, and total involvement.

The meaning of a ceremony is often not implicit in what is observed. Rather, the meaning is something that is learned and acquired both directly and indirectly. If we were to depend entirely upon rational examination of the ceremonial process, we would find that we could not be helped much in our understanding. If we were to watch a group of people taking communion or attending Mass, we would find it difficult to make any sense of what we are observing. In fact, much of it would seem quite stupid. For a bunch of grown-up people to parade around making a big thing out of a tiny wafer and a sip of wine would seem senseless. But for people who understand the symbolism and enter into the ceremonial process with thoughtful intent, the service can be one of the more meaningful moments of worship.

Much of life is made up of little rituals that are so much a part of everyday activity that we do not begin to realize their origin or appreciate their meaning. For instance, when we are introduced to a stranger, one of the first things we do is extend an open palm for a handshake and say, "How do you do?" Can you think of a more meaningless question? "What do you do?" perhaps, or "Where do you come from?" but "How do you do?" Do what? Do whom? But the nonsense question has been filled with meaning as the proper opening gambit in a human encounter, and so we accept it—not for its exact meaning—but rather for its implicit meaning.

Those who are skilled at understanding human behavior can start with a simple handshake and begin to add insight and meaning. The limp handshake means one thing, and the firm grip another. The clammy handshake says something quite different from the dry palm. The warm and cordial greeting is expressed in one way, and the reserved and hostile approach shows up in another. Both are easily interpreted by the person who has had some practice.

Some rituals seem quite unreasonable, and yet they are so socially meaningful that they are a part of life. Imagine the three hundred thousand fans who gather around the Indianapolis Speedway to watch drivers risk life and limb tearing around a track hour after hour. Imagine tennis fans watching as sweating people endlessly bat a ball back and forth over a net. Or imagine eleven professional bruisers assembled in battle array to assault eleven similar representatives of institutions of higher learning. For what purpose? Not to establish intellectual superiority, but rather to move a piece of inflated animal hide around a carefully manicured expanse of lawn for an hour or so. Nonrational, of course, but the meaning is not in the reason but in the acquired sense of what is important in the ritualized acting-out.

This acquired meaning can be used for fun and games, or it can be employed for important therapeutic purposes—such as the acting out of the deep emotions of acute grief. What at first might seem like an absurd process may be the most important form of emotional release that is available to the distressed persons. Lawrence Abt indicates that these ceremonies give people a chance to act out feelings that are too deep to be put into words. When looked at in this light, the apparently meaningless begins to take on a new perspective and quite a different value.

The meaning is acquired out of a need to cope with the deeper feelings of life. Here—probably more so than in most conditions of human communication—the medium is the message. The ceremonial process tells something important to those who are initiated into the social significance of ceremonies. When one rides past a church and sees many decorated cars and a woman in a long white flowing gown, no one has to be told there is going to be a wedding. Everyone knows that, and part of the message is that there is almost universal acceptance of the nature and meaning of the event.

Similarly, a long row of black cars following a special car filled with flowers and another special type of motor coach tells everyone that someone has died, and that what is going on is a funeral, a ceremony designed to help meet the needs of those who are in grief. The message is acted out in such a way that there is instant recognition of the process. Part of the importance of the ceremonial acting-out is that there is a minimum need for explanation. Those who choose to participate, do so knowing that they are part of an all-encompassing process that needs no words to interpret it.

The reason that ceremonies carry the type of message they do is that people have difficulty putting their thoughts and feelings into words unless there are forms of ritualized expression to help say it for them. The more emotional the stress surrounding a human event, the more most people have difficulty putting their thoughts and feelings into words. The ritualized behavior comes in handy because it makes it easier to become part of a supportive group. The funeral is a time for sharing and communicating group support. It is a time for acting out the feelings that may be difficult to put into words.

Ceremonial processes are usually rich in symbolism. In the symbolic forms of expression, a variety of nonverbal ways of expressing feelings come into play. The wedding uses special attire, special music, special decorations, special settings, and special words. The varied forms of language that are the function of art add to the meaning of mere words the special significance that should be attributed to the event.

Every culture, from the most primitive to the most

71

sophisticated, seems to use these forms of ritualized expression to surround important events. In the national and political forms of ceremony, there is almost always the stirring music and precision marching of military bands, which, as a form of unified dance and patriotic song, are designed to stimulate feelings fitting for the occasion. All these modes of communication combine to generate feelings of pride and security—so important in building national trust and willingness to sacrifice for the common good.

The group process is vitally important to group life, especially when there are life crises. The ceremony gives an opportunity for expressing the feelings of the group in some organized and accepted way. Everyone senses the meaning and message of the event and, in effect, finds it an easy way of joining in and saying, "Those are my sentiments too."

A form of social insurance exists in group life. When those with special needs are supported by the group, they obligate themselves to return the support at other times. For instance, those who attend a funeral and visitation are saying to the immediately bereaved, "You were doing this for me a few years ago when my emotional need was great. Now I am coming to your support when you need me." But there is more to it than that, for indirectly the communication says: "I am the living evidence that it is possible to meet grief and move through it. Although it may seem unbearable at the time, there is a healing process that comes about slowly, and I verify it for you because I have survived and may be stronger because of my experience."

The group process also creates the atmosphere within which it is proper and valid to express the appropriate emotions. When emotions are repressed, they find detours that may be a threat to health. When they are expressed in adequate form, the release may have important therapeutic value. So the group support provides what may not be available in any other way.

The ceremonial process also provides a form of total involvement that is important for working through the powerful emotions. To try to cope with strong feelings through a limited process such as intellectualization may do

72

more harm then good, for the denial of feelings may lead to their repression and adverse forms of acting out, or rather acting in. Much illness apparently can be traced to the unwise handling of feelings by various forms of denial.

The ceremonial process affirms feelings, and encourages the total expression of the person to what is happening in life. Therefore, most ceremonies are centered about physical, mental, emotional, and spiritual forms of expression.

Most ceremonies are also centered about large-muscle activity, since it provides a way of involving the body in emotional expression. This is important because it gives nature a chance to act out feelings through the normal forms of coping—for example, excess glandular secretion. Many ceremonies involve a parade, a social form of muscle activity that can be easily adapted to the occasion.

Ceremonies also have an emotional setting. They provide a variety of emotional stimuli that make it possible for the feelings that are close to the surface, but have been blocked by inhibitions and apprehensions, to come forth. Unblocking the impacted feelings may be the most important immediate task for those who are so caught up in grief that their more normal modes of expression are paralyzed.

In our culture, ceremonies are often entrusted to the religious institution, which gives an intellectual and spiritual perspective to what has happened. It uses philosophical and theological insight to fit the individual event into man's history and to satisfy his need to understand both the meaning and the message that is implicit in the event.

The oldest known evidence of ceremonial activity in the history of man is the remnants of a funeral event that occurred in Persia sixty thousand years ago. Archaeologists have unearthed the remains of an ancient burying ground in Sanidar. Here they found human remains carefully covered with elk shoulder blades for protection. Buried with the bodies was seed, which was interpreted to mean a belief in immortality and the need for food in the next existence. Also found were concentrated little piles of what proved to be pollen, the remains of floral tributes that had been left with the bodies. All in all, we have here the basic constituents of the funeral process—burial with ceremony and verification of ideas that give cosmic perspective to individual death.

Through the sixty thousand intervening years, there has been a constant need to verify the value of life and to confront openly and honestly the impact of physical death. Philippe Ariès had described these processes in the history of Christendom, and he shows how the attitude toward life is reflected in the practices that are employed at the time of death. When life has been highly valued, the funeral process gives significance to the person who has died, and surrounds the ceremonial events with dignity and meaning. When life has lost its social significance, the funeral ceremonies are minimized or eliminated altogether, as with the barbarities of the Nazi prison camps.

If the funeral is an index of cultural attitudes, it is important for us to assess the trends of our day in relation to the acting-out processes incident to the death of an individual. Two trends are evident. One would reduce or eliminate ceremonial acting-out, clearly a reflection of the secularized and antipersonal mood of our day. The other would build upon the discoveries of researchers and therapists in supporting the need to wisely manage the deep feelings of grief and use the possibilities of the funeral process for that purpose.

Persons working on the reevaluation of the funeral as a therapeutic resource have defined an eight-step process that is designed to meet the emotional, social, intellectual, and spiritual needs of people. These eight steps would make it possible for the best insights of research to be implemented in a way that can give group support, aid in confronting reality, and also provide the emotional climate needed to express deep feelings.

The eight steps involve—first—a verifiable death. Work with missing-in-action relatives indicates that it is difficult to start the healthful process of mourning without verification of the death of the individual who is mourned. To start a funeral process without evidence of death is as difficult as waiting endlessly for the verification that would seem to warrant the working through of the deep feelings.

Second is the process of notification of all who have a relationship to the deceased so that they may share in the funeral process and experience its therapeutic benefits. This would include professional persons, colleagues, friends, and relatives. It would utilize telephone, newspaper, radio, and other channels of communication to alert all who are concerned.

Third would be the verification of confrontation. This, according to Erich Lindemann, is the most important part of the funeral process, because it breaks through denial more effectively than anything else and starts the true work of mourning. This moment of truth should be in a private setting, like the funeral home, where conversation and expression of feelings can be encouraged without embarrassment.

Fourth is the support of the sustaining community—the family, friends, parishioners, and colleagues. Here they share in the confronting of reality and thereby confirm it. They help to create the climate in which real feelings are expressed rather than denied.

Fifth is the religious ceremony, wherein eyes are turned away from the physical remains so that spiritual resources can be verified and used as a resource for moving beyond the past into the future, where the rest of life must be lived. This is a time for education concerning the spiritual nature of all life and the value of spiritual resources. These moments can help all persons to confront the reality of death and its meaning for those still alive. It can give a chance to do anticipatory grief work at the same time that it helps others do some of their unfinished grief work. It is a testimony to the value of life; for while the funeral is for the benefit of those who are still alive, it affirms that a life has been lived and valued, and in so doing, it enhances the value of all life.

The sixth step is the final disposition of the physical remains. The interment completes the process of dealing with the physical aspects of death, but at the same time it verifies the promises of the resurrection; for as the grain of wheat falls to the ground, it creates the possibility for growth a hundredfold. When cremation is chosen, it should not be used as a device for eliminating the funeral process; rather, it should function only as an alternative to the burial in the earth. The therapeutic value of the funeral process should not be given up.

Seventh would be some form of ceremonial reentry for those who are acutely bereaved. This might be a return home for some form of group sharing, or perhaps a return to the church. It might involve special recognition for the family at the next Sunday's service. In effect, it is an effort to stay with the acutely bereaved, rather than an apparent abandonment at the graveside.

Eighth is continued pastoral supervision or other form of professional concern. This is to help the person do some of the important work of mourning that can never be completely finished in the funeral process. Here the sensitive professional or concerned friend can stay with the bereaved until it is clear he has moved back toward the mainstream of life rather than succumbed to the whirlpool of his grief.

When one considers the psychological movement that is basic to the wise management of acute grief, it becomes clear that the ceremonial acting-out is probably the most available and most valid form of intervention that any community can provide.

8

Grief and Children

The last generation or two have thrown much light on the processes of development in the lives of children. We have been helped to see more clearly what takes place in the emotional life of children. For centuries it had been assumed that not much happened within the lives of children until they were old enough to talk or understand what was going on around them. Now we know that quite the opposite is true. Much goes on that helps to shape the life of a child, well before there is any ability to verbalize or understand the meaning of the events of life or the behavior of other persons.

This is especially true with any event in which the emotional content is great. Children, in their early years, live almost entirely by their emotional sensitivity. Because they cannot understand language, they are highly sensitive to clues they perceive concerning the feelings of others. They are so sensitive to these emotional messages that the messages may play a dominant role in shaping their personality responses for many years to come.

Because much of this early preverbal material of life is communicated by emotions, the rich content of the emotional life of a child may be outside of the norms of communication. This is good if the material makes the child feel secure and loved. It may be damaging if the child feels insecure and threatened. Often it is not so important what is said in the presence of a child as how it is said, that is, what emotional meaning is communicated to the child. When the atmosphere is charged with disturbing emotions, the child may be unable to assess the meaning of the feelings and may arrive at a false interpretation that is quite damaging to his inner being.

The powerful emotions that grief evokes may spill over into the life of a child. While adults may justify their verbalizations by saying, "Of course, he can't understand," they do not appraise the emotional impact of the circumstances that surround the utterance.

Adults may also assume that a child has no capacity for grief. And although it may be quite right that a child has no ability to comprehend the meaning of death, since he has no sense of time and space, it is just this inability that may make his response to acute loss all the more devastating. Children feel that all of life is an extension of their own being. They feel secure in the framework of strong arms and loving tenderness. When this is suddenly withdrawn, their security is shattered, and life is overwhelmed with an all-pervading insecurity.

Since all of life's communications in early months and years are centered in emotional responses, the emotional injury that accompanies loss and dislocation may be devastating. Children who are separated from tender love and care, even though they may have adequate food and medical care, have a much higher death rate than those who are given emotional support but less adequate food and medical care.

A senior in a seminary was referred to a counselor because there were indications he would have trouble working with the bereaved and with conducting funerals. Though he had an excellent record as a student, a pleasant personality, and every evidence of poise and maturity, those who knew him felt he was carrying a heavy burden of death-anxiety.

At the appointed time, the young man appeared at the counselor's office. Soon he was explaining to the counselor that he found it difficult to walk past a funeral home and seemed to panic when he saw a funeral coach. Quite obviously, he would have trouble with funerals. In response to questioning, he said that he had never been to a funeral and that there had never been a death in his family. Exploring to see where the anxiety might have originated, the counselor asked about siblings, mother, and father; and the young man admitted that he knew nothing about his father.

This seemed to be a topic worth pursuing, and in response to more questioning, the young man expressed his uncertainty about the whole matter of his father. He agreed to spend an evening with his mother and ask for all the information he could think of about his father. When he returned to the counseling room the next day, he was quite excited, because he said that he had not only found out a great deal about his father but about his mother as well. In fact, he felt as if he knew her for the first time in his life. He said they talked nearly all night. While the story he told seemed hard to believe, the human dynamics were clear.

The father had been killed in an industrial accident when the young man was sixteen months old. The mother was distraught and tried to shield the child from any of the tragic knowledge. She persuaded herself that he was too young to understand and that when the time was right she would be able to tell him. But she did not take into account her own need, which made her ever more protective. He was her whole life, and she could not bring herself to inflict injury upon him by telling such a sad story.

However, the lad did not live in a vacuum. When he went out to play, other boys talked often of their fathers—about fishing trips, ball games, and visits to the circus. With the boy, it was always a blank spot in life. He learned early that it was a subject about which no questions were to be asked. But the empty spot was not to be ignored. It grew in importance in his life until it seemed to be central. It crowded in upon all sorts of circumstances until it was necessary to repress the feelings that came with it. Death seemed to be the answer, and so his fears about death grew until they were diffused throughout his life.

His education and his vocational choice seemed to be the part of his quest for answers that never came. Now, in a long and fruitful evening, he had found the answers that made it possible for him to grow in understanding and competence for facing life. It was also important for his understanding of the needs of others and his role in ministering to those needs. What might have been a nightmare was transformed into a resource for growth and ministry. Early childhood experience can determine the course of life, and concerned intervention can prevent a painful injury from becoming a lifelong obsession.

It becomes important for us to have a clear understanding of the way a child's mental and emotional life develops. Too often we think of a child as a small adult, and we approach his life with a concern that emerges from the adult's perspective. This may be difficult for both the adult and the child.

The developmental process in the growth of a child's concepts can be seen clearly in his understanding of grief.

A young child, from birth to about three years of age, has little or limited language facility. The capacity to remember seems to be closely linked with the ability to use verbal forms. Most people, therefore, cannot remember much that happened to them before they were three years old. But that does not mean that many significant events having a bearing on the basic attitude toward life have not been taking place.

A young child is incapable of having a concept of death, because time and space ideas have not been developed yet. We need to be able to think in terms of finality or some terminal event in order to think of death. But the life of a child is centered in the now because of his feelings of need and relationship. When these central needs are dislocated, there can be strong feelings. That explains why a child can have a tremendous sense of grief without having any "idea" of death.

When the child's small world of experience, of which he is the center, is dislocated, feelings of threat and insecurity can overwhelm him. The child is so completely dependent that nothing seems more devastating to his world than abandonment. When death removes someone important in the child's life, the response is a sense of loss compounded by fear, insecurity, unresolved pain, and a sense of abandonment.

This gives us some clues as to how to respond to the child's grief. Explanations and verbal reassurance are not closely related to what is going on in the child, and so are apt to be worthless. What the child needs is related to the sense of loss that is paramount in his awareness. He needs to have the tender love and care that can make him feel he is not abandoned. He needs the attentions that can move him back into the center of the picture, with play as he understands it and love as he interprets it.

These early needs of the child become a permanent part of the human response to acute loss. In times of great stress, therefore, and as long as he lives, he will respond positively to those who pay attention to his needs and treat him with the understanding and care that relieve the pains deep within.

When a child becomes older, from four to seven (and one can never be too precise about these delineations, since children are people, and people differ in many ways), the focus of his response to death changes. He has developed greater facility with words, but is trying to fill out the meaning of the words he hears and uses. His experience has changed, and he is busy with the tasks of relating words and events to the language he is discovering.

During these years, he is more active, and he explores his world; but he is also still the center of much of this outward activity, and he is strangely preoccupied with himself and his body. He wants to know how it works and how it feels. He wants to know also about other people's bodies and how they work. So he explores himself inside and out. Quite naturally, his concern about death will have biological dimensions.

Many of the questions children of this age will ask about death will take this form of biological curiosity, for they are trying to build a concept of death that fits well biologically into their growing ideas of both life and death. They will investigate dead things like birds and cats. They will try to discover the difference between death and life.

Should a person close to them die, they may ask all manner of questions related to this effort to know the meaning of physical death. Some of the questions may seem inappropriate to the adults around, but not to the child. He may ask, "How do you eat when you are dead?" or "How do you go to the bathroom when you are dead?" These have been important concerns in his life, and he now tries to relate them to the concept of death.

He may show that he knows a person is dead and buried, but he still may not be clear as to the nature of sensory processes. So the questions he asks are likely to be efforts to sharpen his understanding on this point. He may ask, "If I yell loud enough, can Grandma hear me?" or "If I jump on her grave will it hurt her?" He knows his grandmother is buried, but he has difficulty thinking of life without a sensory response; so he is working at the process of developing a clearer idea of what it means to be dead.

During this period, it is important to give very accurate and simple answers to the questions asked. Efforts to overanswer or underanswer are apt to be interpreted by the youngster as anxiety; and he needs fact, insight, and honest answers—not anxiety—at this stage of his development. But because of the cumulative nature of personality development, it may also be important for him to have tender love and care and a sensitivity to his needs as he explores these new areas of his understanding. This may be a time to use the educational opportunities afforded to make him careful to protect his life and be careful of the lives of others.

When a child becomes more of a social creature, it is quite natural that his interest in death will change. As he grows out into a world of schools and community activity, he will broaden his experience and interests. His sense of time and space will develop to the extent that he will know more people and be able to observe the social relationships that bind people together.

The area of his exploration will reflect this growing interest. When a neighbor dies he may ask, "Who will take care of the Jones children now that their father is dead?" or "What will happen to Mrs. Smith now that she is all alone?" These questions grow out of a sense of human relationship, and they need to be answered in that context.

It may be characteristic of this age that the child will want to talk about matters involving death. Especially if the deceased was someone close to him, so that his own sense of relationship is involved, he may want to explore what is going on in his world of thought and experience. This process will usually become evident at ages eight to eleven, depending upon the individual child.

As the eight-to-eleven age bracket is a time when important insights into the meaning of life and its management are taking place, it is wise to assess the educational possibilities of the child's invitation to talk about life and death. This is a time when the effort is made to make sense of life, to discover what is valid and appropriate in self-discovery and social relations. Thus it is important to be completely honest, yet reassuring. The child needs to be assured that he has some major responsibility for his own life, and that if he is careful, he will have a better chance for a healthy life than if he is careless.

The child at this age may be seeking some answers to the questions that baffle him about when, why, and how death is experienced in life. It seems more valid for older people to die than young people. It seems more valid for people who have been sick for a long time to die than it does for an apparently well person. It seems that there is more personal pain in grief when death is tragic and untimely than when it comes at the end of a long and useful life. So in response to the asked or unasked question, it is important to give the child at this age reassurance without deceit. An adult may say at the appropriate time, "Of course, there is always an element of life that is unpredictable, but we expect to be around for a long time yet. We expect to see you grow up, graduate from college, and have children of your own. Yes, we think we would make good grandparents. But we also know that each of us has to live wisely, because we have a lot to do with how things go in life."

This form of reassurance is educational, for it asserts the child's responsibility for his own health and behavior. Cause-effect factors are kept in focus, and no adult assumptions of omnipotence get in the way of honest and reasonable explanations.

But when the problem of the child is related to the death of someone important in his life, there will also be a need for love and care and honest answers to questions about the nature of the accidental and the problems of illness. The physical and the emotional needs still exist, even though the child at this age is adding the social dimension to his understanding of life processes and death experiences.

The teen-ager has moved into the more complete capacity for abstract ideas, and he may want to talk about death or his death apprehensions in terms of his psychological, philosophical, and spiritual concerns. In fact, the adolescent's talking may be a form of experimental living, whereby he moves into an abstract world to see if he can understand the feelings that go along with it.

If the adolescent has a backlog of death-anxiety that has been planted in earlier years, this may be the time when it is acted out in irrational and often self-threatening behavior. The adolescent may approach his anxiety by trying to prove to himself that he is not really afraid of death. So he may risk his life in order to allay his fears. Often this proves to be a tragic form of behavior; reckless driving of a car or destructive use of drugs can have devastating consequences.

But adolescence is also a time of heroic challenges and self-dedication. This is the time when noble visions for life may be created. The idealism of this stage of life has been the basis for vocational commitments that set the course of life for years to come. This is the time when ideals for life are set and acted out in the choice of a life partner, a philosophy of life, and a vocation. How important it is, then, that the needs for a healthful attitude toward life and death be built into the life-experience of the teen-ager.

This is the time when it is important to develop a discriminating attitude toward life and death. Some death is tragic, and some is noble. Some death is a fulfillment of life, and some death is a frustration of the best in life. Also, it is important to develop a response to the deep feelings about life and death. Some ways of managing grief are self-destructive and futile, and others may make a person more competent and mature. The opportunity to grow in understanding may be developed at this time through explorations of the self and the relationships that can enrich life.

When a person has grown through the developmental process to this stage, he should have a well-rounded attitude toward life and death that includes tender love and care, biological understanding, social perspectives, and a healthy philosophy of life. When any part of the developmental process has been neglected, it may show up in adult behavior. When the growth process has been wisely managed in all of its dimensions, the adult should be competent to cope with even the most distressing aspects of life and death.

But there are some things that we should always keep in mind when dealing with children. First, we should try to understand where they are in terms of their emotional development. This is basic for meaningful communication. Second, we should realize that it may be possible to confuse children by misinformation, but that children have built-in lie detectors and can sense when they are being deceived. They will quickly lose confidence in those dishonest persons to whom they must nevertheless turn for guidance and understanding. Also, it is important to realize that children want to participate in family ceremonies and are never too young to share in a funeral designed to show the value of life. But should a child not want to participate in a funeral, it is a danger signal; for it shows that the child has already picked up anxiety about death, and this will be an important concern in working through the child's apprehension about the rites that accompany death.

Children have a lot of life left to live, so it is important to guide them in such a way that they develop wise and healthful attitudes toward their feelings, their lives, and their deaths.

9

Grief and the Aged

Quite a different set of circumstances exist when we compare the grief of the aged with that of the child. The child is at the threshold of life. The future lies ahead, and what happens in childhood may have a bearing on the course of life for years to come.

The aged person has lived life and knows by the relentless course of time that death is a real possibility for the near future. In fact, in projective testing of persons over fifty, Herman Feifel found that the major unconscious preoccupation of the persons in that age group was their own death. While they might carefully avoid mention of the subject, and make vigorous efforts to keep it from entering their minds, the fact remained that they knew the simple mathematics of the human life-span and sooner or later had to face up to its meaning.

Sometimes there was active denial and an effort to pretend they had drunk of the waters of eternal youth. This may lead to what appears to be foolish and unreasonable behavior. At other times, there was a morbid preoccupation with death and a constant effort to share the apprehension with others. At still other times, there was an effort to gain a wiser perspective on life and to develop the inner resources to strengthen the spiritual life.

The aged occasionally make fun of their advanced years.

One gentleman in his nineties explained to me that he was very glad he had made it safely to the nineties. With a twinkle in his eye, he said that he read the obituaries in the *New York Times* every day and found that very few people died in their nineties so it must be the safest age. Other old people speak of the hills that have suddenly risen up along familiar walkways, and of the fact that they have to use their brains more because they can use their muscles less. They make fun of the signs of partial death by explaining that their memory is just as good as it ever was, but that now they remember different things. And the impairment of physical function is oftentimes the focal point of humor. And gravity is given credit for its final victory, as all of the elements of life begin to sag.

In many ways the grief of the adult is part and parcel of his stage of development. He has had more time to make an emotional investment in the life of another, and when death comes to that important other, there may be a loss of meaning for life. So much of the self has been involved in the life of the other that death severely diminishes the self that is doing the grieving. This means that a large degree of resignation and despair may overwhelm the bereaved person, and life may, for awhile at least, seem too much of a burden to carry. It is at this point that we see the significance of Erik Erikson's distinction between integrity and despair as major characteristics of the aging person. The loss of the major love-object may precipitate despair, and along with it feelings of low self-esteem, suspicion of others, and a sense of unresolved restlessness. It is as if nothing can ever be right again.

In order to understand the nature of the grief response among aged persons, it is important to look at some of the experiences that tend to be a part of the life of aging people in our culture. More so than in any other time in history, perhaps, the aged are segregated, isolated, and abandoned. Their personal and social needs appear to be more adequately met at one level of life and ignored at another.

Social security has given some financial benefits to many persons, but it has also tended to create some psychological and emotional problems that have to be taken into account when plotting the adjustments the aged must make in modern culture. As they approach the magic age of sixty-five, a subtle change comes about in the lives of many persons. When they make their pilgrimage to the social security office to register for their pension and medicare, they mark a major turning point in life. They move from the ranks of the gainfully employed to the roles of the aged—as society defines them. Whether or not they make this form of self-assessment, they are obliged to face the fact that the social patterns for their lives are going to change. For many, this event means the termination of the employment that has given their lives meaning, structure, and value in the past. For many, it is clearly a rite of passage.

This rite of passage appears to have demographic implications. In our society it has been quite common for men to marry women who are younger than they are. This may be due to the more rapid maturation of women, as well as to the longer period of time required for a man to complete his education and training and achieve economic stability, often a prerequisite for marriage. The inequity of marriage age is compounded by the fact that life expectancy for men is now sixty-eight and for women seventy-six. So the eight years difference in life expectancy is added to the age variables at the time of marriage. Then the enforced retirement of many men is often not matched by that of women, since many women have worked only in the home, and will continue to do so long after they are sixty-five. The loss of status in the life of the man may cause identity problems that are acted out in such a way that life becomes disturbed emotionally and physically. So we have the gap of life further extended and the percentage of widows to widowers becoming quite out of proportion.

The social and emotional dislocation that is experienced by widows is one of the major problems of our culture, not only because it exists, but because its existence is so consistently ignored. The social, economic, and emotional plight of the grieving widow makes her vulnerable to a number of stresses that have health implications. A study at Harvard conducted by Dr. Phyllis Silverman produced the figure that widows are 700 percent more apt to die the first year after the death of a husband than other women of comparable age groups. Were any other group shown to be that vulnerable, there would be a national committee to study the matter, with endowments being given to support dramatic forms of intervention. But the plight of the widow continues to be largely ignored. And the activity of the government seems to be in the opposite direction; the FTC works to destroy the effectiveness of the most prevalent and therapeutic forms of intervention available to the acutely bereft. Bureaucratic action may well eliminate the most useful parts of the funeral process.

The distinction Erikson makes between integration and despair tells much of the story of life as aged persons experience it. What happens during these late years sums up all of the years that came before, both in terms of what has been learned about the wise handling of life and its problems and the frustration and defeat that may well be the end result instead. A life that has moved from one distressing experience to another without ever learning anything really significant from them is likely to climax in despair.

Erikson points out that many persons fail to find value and meaning in the experience of the now. They are inclined to blame failure on the past. Their inability to function has been attributed to heredity, environment, inadequate parents, or any other of the elements of the past that can be used as scapegoats. If they cannot blame the past, they tend to blame the future; and they continually approach life overcome with fears of failure and apprehensions about what people will think or say. Thus they do not use the opportunities of the present to become the persons they could well be.

For the aged person, the future has come, and all of the accumulation of failures that have made up their past become the resources they have to work with in the present. If the now has never served them well, if they have never been able to enjoy being alive when and where they are, the prospects for retirement are gloomy indeed; for it will inevitably be more of the same. The problems of aging and retirement are not so much external as they are internal. If a person has spent a lifetime developing skills in failure, they will be hard to replace when he is his own boss and must set the course of his own life.

But it need not be that way. The alternative Erikson presents is one of achieving integrity of being. This is the bringing together of the fruits of life in a courageous and inner-directed expression of being. As in a piece of music, all of the themes are brought together in a *coda* or masterly *stretto* that fulfills the best of the self.

But this achievement of selfhood, at its best, is not apt to happen unless there is a long and careful period of preparation. A person has to develop trust in himself. He must believe that the gift of life can be filled with experiences both good and ill that can contribute to genuine self-realization. To this end, the inner-directed person seeks out the best meaning of whatever happens in life. In the end instead of causing bitterness and frustration, hostility and despair, the integrative process can bring together the long and fruitful experience of life in a period of enjoyment and satisfaction.

Then, retirement and the prospect of dying will not be so fraught with anxiety. Rather, they can be inspirations for doing the important unfinished tasks of life in preparation for the next adventure, which may well be the climax of a spiritual pilgrimage. Nothing is more pathetic than a person who runs out of life before he is dead, and is simply waiting around for the final physical event. Few things are more challenging than the life that is taken tiptoe to the very last.

The grief of the person who has integrated life will be quite a different thing from that of the person who has built up a backlog of frustration and despair. Where anxiety and despair dominate life, the threat of death or the experience of bereavement may be so threatening that it causes life to fall apart. The inner world of the despairing person may have been held together by the strength of another, and when that other dies, there may be little left except the pain and the distress.

Quite in contrast, the person who has grown in faith and coping skills will be apt to accept those events as incidental to our mortal natures, and to adopt a perspective that cooperates with cosmic processes rather than reluctantly capitulates to them.

The person who understands the inevitable may even make an interesting game out of the process of preparation. For instance, a person may derive enjoyment from disposing of the possessions he has acquired and appreciated through life.

When I arrived at that magic milepost of sixty-five, I became aware that the laws of mathematics were telling me something important, and I tried to listen. While I would not hasten the process—for enjoyment of life is still important for me—I would rather add to that enjoyment through the joy of skillful giving.

For thirty years I have been collecting first editions of books that I think have special value. Many of these have been autographed by the author or been inscribed by their former owners—sometimes rather significant persons. I have enjoyed finding these books, reading them, and experiencing the satisfaction of possessing what to me are extensions of the personalities of important people. The books afforded me intellectual companionship in a more highly personalized way than could otherwise have been possible.

Now I am enjoying trying to find younger persons who may enjoy and treasure these books as much as I have. So I am engaged in a game that I find quite thrilling. When I meet with younger persons, I try to find out their literary interests. Then I go through a mental checklist of the five hundred or more books I have in my collection of first editions. A young man told me he had written his dissertation on Jonathan Edwards. When I returned home, I wrapped and put in the mail a first edition of his sermons. Now this young man is a special friend, and has a possession that is uniquely satisfying to him.

Another young friend said that he had started collecting first editions and already had two Arthur Conan Doyle firsts. When I sent him four more, he acted as if I had given him a mortgage on the White House, and I had the enjoyment of sharing his enjoyment. Over the last few years I have played this game with ever-widening circles of satisfaction; for I am dispersing the treasure I know I cannot take with me at the same time I am making others the caretakers of my possessions. Just as I enjoyed acquiring these rare books, I am enjoying (even more) the satisfaction that comes with giving them away.

While there are some things that can be done to ease the aging experience, it is important to realize that aging seems to be a physically irreversible process. While the time factor may vary, the end result is always the same.

The cyclic nature of the aging process has long been associated with a second childhood; and the more we study the process, the more apt this characterization seems to be. Young children are completely dependent upon others for the essential care of their bodies and their lives. This is also often true of the aged.

Young children have difficulty with communication, and their sensory awareness has limitations. The aged also may have limited senses; they may be deaf or suffer from some paralysis of the speech so that they have difficulty relating to others. This tends to cause retreat into the inner world of being, a response that is so important for the child during the early months of life.

Young children have difficulty eating, and they often have to live on special diets that are adapted to their toothless state. So also the aged are often without teeth that are adequate, or they have digestive conditions that call for special foods. Both the young child and the aged person often have to be spoon-fed.

Young children are not able to dress themselves and often rebel against the use of clothes. So too with those at the other end of the life cycle. Children have no capacity for reasoning, and often this seems to be true of the aged. The young child has areas of heightened sensitivity, and this may also be true of the aged, who become more sensitive to things that would not have bothered them in their middle years.

One could continue to make comparisons of the relationship of the physical, mental, and emotional conditions that mark both the first and second childhoods. But it is clear enough that similarities exist. These similarities may be significant for understanding the grief response of those who are aged. Often the response is muted by the changes in mental and emotional capacities.

Because of serious physical conditions that required day and night nursing care, my father was placed in a nursing home. After a couple of months, my mother asked if it would be possible for her to be with him in the same home. They were moved into a room that they were able to share, and at first there seemed to be companionship and satisfaction in being together. But as the months passed, each seemed to become increasingly preoccupied with the essentials of care for the alimentary canal and the other basic life-support systems. When my father finally died quietly in his sleep, my mother made no comment about his absence. Never once in the next two years of her life did she make any reference to his life or his death. While in most ways her mind seemed clear, the affective capacity seemed to have withered away, and evidences of any normal forms of grief seemed to be absent.

While this more extreme reduction of emotional response may not be typical, the general reduction of life-energies and life-interests appears to reduce the capacity for normal grief.

Specialized forms of grief response may be observed with the aged as with children. While children lack verbal capacity to talk much about their feelings, they may act them out in clear and specific ways. Gorer traced much youthful vandalism to the acting out of feelings of anger and injustice against the physical symbols of authority. The aged may use other (and for them more appropriate) forms of acting out.

Some studies show that the aged develop physical symptoms to act out the feelings they find difficult to express. They may have a marked reduction of sensory awareness. They may become hard of hearing or hard of seeing. In effect, they consciously or unconsciously reduce the stimuli that might add to their distress. This is part of their retreat into the inner world, where they can live by themselves and limit the obligations and burdens of living.

For some there are signs of reduced activity, especially in the muscles and joints. There may be stiffness and aches that reduce the desire to walk. There may be rheumatic pains and arthritis, which also limit movement. There may be a retreat to a wheelchair, which becomes the aged equivalent of the baby carriage.

While these may be the more morbid manifestations of the acting out of grief among the aged, there may be more healthful ways of doing it. The time and nature of the withdrawal process may be a form of cloture on life-experience. The aged person may withdraw into himself to go back over the choice memories of life. There may be a recall of the important events of childhood, and when conversation is employed, there is apt to be a preponderant amount of childhood recollection. There may be a recall of pleasant memories of youth and love. There may be a rehearsing of the emotions of parenthood. When a person has an accident, a whole lifetime of experience may flash through his consciousness. The aged person may have a similar experience, except that the process is deliberate and drawn out, and it may be filled with deep pleasure.

The aged person may have muted responses to life, but the responses that do exist need to be understood and attended to adequately. The aged who enjoy their families should not be abandoned. Just as those in a comatose state have limited capacities to respond, so there seems to be a residue of sensory awareness that is able to respond automatically to other people. If there is satisfaction in knowing other people care, there may be just as significant an awareness of abandonment and rejection.

As with any other period of life, needs exist. While the needs may be curtailed and conditioned by circumstance, persons who care may well pay attention to old persons' responses. We must remember that children are people, and the aged are people. Our efforts to understand the meaning of the movement inward should not blind us to the need for sustaining social contact, even if its potential is clearly more limited.

In our efforts to be aware of the nature of the grief of the aged and their deep needs, we should work to reduce despair and to make even these final moments of life a time of integration.

10

Grief and Religion

The question is often raised, "Does a person's religion make any difference in the way he experiences grief?" The answer, of course, must be that it depends on the religion of the person. As William James pointed out long ago, there is healthy religion and there is unhealthy religion. Some religious attitudes help life to grow, and some stunt personality growth.

The kind of religion that tends to reduce resources for coping with death realistically is usually centered about the denial of responsibility, the distortion of reality, and the creation of illusory concepts of the person and the universe.

The religious escape from responsibility tends to stunt personality growth. It projects a concept of the universe as uncertain, capricious, and easily open to manipulation. It takes the nature of the baby and projects it endlessly, so that the person who cries loud and long is able to produce cosmic results and a cosmic parent will then violate the law and order of the universe to care for him. Such an attitude will undermine the disciplined growth that is necessary for becoming a responsible person.

When Jesus set out on his ministry, his first task was to come to terms with his sense of responsibility. When he made his first public announcement of his ministry, he made it clear that he was respecting the cause-effect processes of the universe and affirmed, "The spirit of the Lord is upon me *because* . . ."

In order to prove to himself that he had achieved this necessary form of responsibility toward himself and the universe, he took some time for intensive self-preparation. He went to a quiet place and carefully examined his assumptions about life. Was he going to use spiritual power to violate natural law? He told himself clearly he was not. He would not violate the order of molecular structure by changing a stone into a loaf of bread just because he was hungry.

Nor would he violate the law of gravity just to prove that he was special in the structure of the universe. So he would not jump off of the roof of the temple to attract attention by being spectacular. Rather he chose to follow the more demanding example of the Cross. In this way he could better establish the values that were important in his thinking. Later, and in another context, he made it clear that he would function within the law and order of the universe; for he respected the Creator of the natural order.

Jesus would not violate the laws of social relationship either. If people hated and destroyed God's revelation, he would not bargain with truth in order to have limited political and social power. He would not sell his soul or compromise his integrity in order to have an easy but partial victory in this life. Instead, he chose the course of slow but valid process—a demonstration of personal commitment. In the long run, this would be closer to cosmic truth than political manipulation.

All during his life Jesus held true to this determination, maintaining his responsibility, as a creature, to respect the law and order of the created universe. He realized the power of God expressing itself in all creation, but it was an uncommitted power waiting for the responsible individual to use it in responsible ways. He said that the sun shone on the just and the unjust, and that the rain fell on the wise as well as the foolish. The responsibility for the use of cosmic resources rested upon the value system of the individual. God made the resources available, and the person determined how they would be used.

The Gospel of John makes it clear that the nature of God was perceived in terms of energy. God is love, God is light, God is power, God is spirit, God is truth. These are the uncommitted power resources of creation waiting to be spiritualized and used by the God-aware individual. This involves no game of trying to manipulate God for personal favors. That would be the ultimate form of sacrilege. Rather, it was a quest for an inner perfection and dedication that would be willing and able to function within the laws of the universe for those purposes that could be in accord with God's will.

Yet, too often the plan that has been revealed through the life of Christ has placed too great a demand on people, and their response has been to escape from it. Thus arises a concept of a manageable universe and a trivialized idea of God as a cosmic errand boy or scapegoat for human failure. So what have we done to the noble revelation?

Too often we have rejected it. We sing lustily, "What a friend we have in Jesus, all our sins and griefs to bear." From one point of view, it would be a poor friend who would want to heap all his songs and griefs on another. And, from another point of view, it is a tragic denial of the New Testament revelation to want to escape from personal responsibility.

Much of our attitude toward death, as it has emerged from religious perceptions, has been to escape responsibility for both life and death. True and healthy religion should be an inspiration to disciplined and responsible living. It should help people grow to the extent that they can take charge of their own lives and live them so that they reduce the causes of guilt and understand the processes necessary for the wise management of grief.

All one has to do to gain some idea of the perversion of the New Testament revelation as it relates to matters of life and death is to listen carefully to the things that may be said at a funeral. A pastor may claim that God's will lies behind the most brutal and cruel events of life. A pastor may pray as if some cosmic entity were just waiting for the orders for the day. The implication is that God had better get busy with his godly business, or man will be obliged to punish him by his rejection. Such trivialization of the nature of God would be likely to separate persons from the ultimate resources they need at the time their need is greatest.

The attitude that is often expressed at funerals is that people are helpless to cope with life and so need a special supply of cosmic kindness to help out on special occasions. This often leads the pastor to promise more than is reasonable, and this leads to disillusionment and a further retreat into unproductive religious practice.

It serves no valid or useful purpose to destroy the New Testament's revelation of the nature of God in order to present a puny religious concept that makes people feel inadequate to confront honestly the needs and experiences of their own living.

When people try to live within the cause-effect framework of life with a clear awareness of their responsibility and an understanding of their resources, they can grow sufficiently in spiritual power to become masters of life through the revelation of Christ. They will then not be obliged to crawl through life begging for what is already theirs if they would only stand to their full stature and accept it.

The Beatitudes present a program for accepting the resources of the universe through disciplined, mature, and responsive behavior. They point out in a series of paradoxes how people can develop the reciprocal skills that can lead to the highest form of self-realization.

In the matter of managing grief, this is explicit. Jesus does not say that there is a special blessedness for those who are in grief. He knew the meaning of grief and loss. He un-ashamedly wept when his friend Lazarus died. But he just as unashamedly helped the sisters of Lazarus to do the healthy work of mourning. And it was this mourning that brought their brother and his friend back to life in a more valid and eternal perception of the indestructible qualities of the God-endowed spirit.

In the Beatitudes, Jesus looks beyond the fact of death and the pain of grief to the healing process of mourning. He makes it clear that those who learn the wise skills of healthful mourning are the ones who emerge with strength. They have accepted the responsibility essential for a mature concept of the universe and its lawful order. They have functioned within that structure of belief to build the spiritual perceptions that are so basic and solid they take on an eternal dimension. (In a later chapter we will consider the idea of immortality, or eternal life.)

If we are committed to the idea of healthful mourning as essential to the strength and comfort of life, how do we see this process of healthful mourning?

In the first place, we would want to stay close to the New Testament model by refusing to deny personal responsibility. We would adhere to the truth that would seek to see and understand things as they are, and would not distort that reality in order to blame others and God for the end results of an orderly process. While we might not like the results of a molecular process or a violation of the law of gravity or the war that follows from political failures, we would not want to destroy reality by asking God to do what is a violation of his nature. We know our human weakness, but we also know that if we are to preserve the majestic concept of the nature of God, we cannot engage in the practices of tempting God to do our will. Instead, it is important for us to discover how we may bring our lives into close accord with that ultimate will.

Seeing death in those terms may well change its meaning for us. The death that causes our inner pain is the death that reduces or diminishes our own meaning for life. If we can understand life's meaning in a larger context, we are then able to see death in a different light. In the book of Job, when the central figure of that drama was overwhelmed with his grief and his friends were not able to meet his needs through their sophistries, the dramatist puts words into the mouth of God; and the substance of these words is that man's limited understanding and his basic selfishness are the causes of much of his grief. Man likes sheep and cattle and does not like crocodiles and rhinoceroses, but that is due to his limited insight—primarily because man cannot use these creatures for his own selfish purposes. But God's plan for creation is larger, and man must grow to understand the larger meaning if he is to achieve mastery of life and grief.

This is especially true of death. Death is as essential to life as life is essential to death. Nothing can die until it has acquired the properties of living matter, and all living matter is in a constant state of being reduced by the basic attrition we call death.

It may be that life is short, as with a moth, or long, as with a Sequoia; but the quality of being alive has implicit in it the quality of dying and knowing death. With humans, the life-span covers a few decades or generations, but we know the built-in plan from the beginning. The only way to outwit death is to avoid the possibility of life in too finite or individual terms.

Yet, even behind the fact of universal death there is a benign factor, for it would be impossible to imagine what life would be like, were there no death. Could we imagine a world in which no one died and the population was glutted with billions of never-dying ancients? It takes young people to guarantee the creation of new life, and the aged must die in order for life to go on. We see the wisdom of this cosmic process in general terms, but it is the individual death that diminishes us and causes the pain of grief.

Our religious faith should help us to find a perspective through which we can evaluate both our own feelings and the ultimate reality that we would not deny. That means that we need to know that all death is not the same. In fact, we are apt to celebrate some death.

On Thanksgiving, for example, the focal point for our celebration is a death. We enjoy the demise of a turkey and surround the event with all manner of symbolic materials or activities. We have the traditional cranberry sauce without stopping to think that the cranberries have been separated from their part in the cosmic process in order to play their special role. The insides of the big bird are filled with stuffing, but little recognition is given to the fact that its visceral life-giving organs have been replaced by a tasty yet nonliving substance that provides nothing more significant than giblet gravy. Yes, it is quite clear that we derive enjoyment from some types of death and even make death the center of a family festival.

101

When we make our trips to the butcher shop, we clearly encourage the processes of death and handsomely pay the agent for this destructive activity. We look into the eyes of the dead salmon and cod with little remorse. Rather, ours is a sense of anticipation; for that form of death is not only acceptable to us but a source of rejoicing. How often have we said, "How I would like to sink my teeth into a good steak"; but how seldom we utter words of this nature with a feeling of grief, guilt, or remorse.

The death that we find valid and acceptable is the kind that does not touch our inner beings with the pain of grief or require the work of mourning. The pain that really touches us is when a part of ourselves dies in the process of another death. When we make an emotional investment in the life of another, we make ourselves vulnerable to the feelings of pain that can come when that other life ends.

In early life, we experience this with pets. These little creatures share our lives—they accept our love and return it. When some tragic event puts an end to them, our feelings are engaged and we suffer. Then when death comes to the neighborhood or the family, we have more intense feelings according to how much our love relationship has been fractured. The essence of grief is the separation experience. Even so, the essence of mourning is the achievement of some form of emotional or spiritual restoration of a relationship.

Healthy religion moves beyond the denial of responsibility, the distortion of reality, and the creating of illusions in order to accomplish some of the important tasks of restoring relationships. Healthy religion helps to put death into perspective. It helps to create a discriminating attitude toward death so that we recognize the meaning of the pain that comes with some death and is absent in others. It helps to undergird life and death with an adequate philosophy, a philosophy that is willing to run the risks of love and accept the penalties of fractured love relationships, but unwilling to allow life to be destroyed in the process.

In the presence of the reality of death, healthy religion emphasizes the reality of life and the unbroken aspects of the relationships that exist in the nonmaterial plane of life.

Without denying the fact of physical death, the undying aspects of other dimensions of living are emphasized so that proper perspectives are maintained.

Healthy religion emphasizes the other forms of love that can continue to sustain life. It points out that only physical things die, and that spiritual things already have the dimension of the infinite and eternal and therefore are indestructible. If God is love, and if those who dwell in love abide in God, then it is unimaginable that God could be self-destructive. What is of God already has the eternal dimension. This perspective may be built into life so deeply that it cushions the impact of physical death and gives a sustaining dimension to life.

Healthy religion also accepts healthy emotions. It does not try to deny feelings, but rather tries to give them the most valid and adequate channels for expression. Perhaps that is why religion has usually provided the ceremonial processes for acting out the deeper feelings of life. Healthy religion does not try to reduce or deny the validity for acting out the deep feelings. Healthy religion would not be found in support of minifunerals any more than it would assume that people can be satisfied with minifeelings.

Healthy religion does not deny or destroy the nature of deep feelings. If grief is the other side of the coin of love, it values the deep feelings that are essential to its existence. Instead of denial, it provides the ways for nurturing the feelings in life and wisely managing them in death.

Healthy religion does not try to deny the processes that are a part of the natural order. Rather, it tries to make it possible for people in grief to appropriate the spiritual insight—and spiritual strength—they need to deal wisely with the events incident to the physical reality.

Healthy religion does not create illusory states and urge people to retreat into them. Its faith was not developed for acts of denial. Rather, it helps people confront reality with openness and honesty and with the sure knowledge that faith is designed to relate to the real rather than to the illusory.

Healthy religion helps people feel at home in the universe as it is. It does not try to re-create the cosmic order by denying what is known about it. The commitment to truth is so basic in healthful religion that it would not try to comfort people by promising what cannot be delivered, or create an artificial universal order that could be manipulated by any devotees of a puny religion.

Healthy religion does not support people's concepts of weakness, nor their dependence upon what is not dependable; rather, it seeks to help people develop the inner courage that makes them strong enough to face reality and cope with it honestly. It is this strength within that is the ultimate resource of those who would live with an inner fortress that makes their souls secure.

Wise and healthy religion, therefore, works to affirm the resources of life. It provides perspective for those times when life-events may distort our view of things. It strengthens faith and courage and makes grace available. Then the promised blessedness is discovered in the very process of wise mourning.

11

Grief and Sex

Probably the two most powerful emotional forces that are at work in human experience are grief over death and the elemental drives related to the procreative, or sexual, impulse.

For several years, I have been a consultant for the program in human sexuality that has been carried on by the medical school of the University of Minnesota. The program was set up originally to help the people in that part of the country face and work through the anxieties and human problems related to human sexuality.

After working with thousands of people and clearly establishing the philosophical base for the program, the researchers discovered that the anxiety most frequently manifested did not have to do with problems of human sexuality but with concern over the meaning of life and death. This involved the need to work through the problems of determining one's self-concept and discovering one's place in the universal order. As the director of the program, Dr. Richard Chilgren, interpreted it, people were coming to the program to find answers to the problems that the church had traditionally provided. But with a new psychology and a new cosmology, the church had abdicated its role, and people had been forced to look elsewhere for the answers.

In this chapter, therefore, we will try to face openly and honestly the areas of life that individually may produce great anxieties and collectively may escalate a person's basic anxieties to the point of breakdown or collapse. We will discuss how adequate insight can be discovered and resources marshaled for the facing of the emotional tasks involved.

Human sexuality fits into a larger form of human relationship. It becomes the basis for the structure of family living, and provides the forms of intimacy and companionship that are not easily created in other human relationships. The very processes of building this type of deep relationship are subtle and all-pervading, so much so in fact that people who have lived together for a number of years would have difficulty explaining what is at work in their lives emotionally. Similarly, it would be equally difficult for them to explain what their emotional needs are when the relationship is broken by death. Human sexuality tends to become the basis for a much deeper and all-pervasive form of interrelationship.

It is the fracturing of this relationship that tends to create the vulnerability experienced by widows and widowers. It is the efforts to heal the fracture that may cause some of the more difficult problems for those who must try to resolve the emotional crisis produced by the death of a spouse.

The problems vary considerably for widows and widowers. And the more satisfactory the marriage that has been fractured, the more difficult may be the problems of resolution. The nature of the problem may well go beyond those areas in which rational processes can usually be employed.

Let us look first at the problem of the widower. With the death of a spouse, the young widower may be faced with the tasks of running a home and raising young children. Not only his basic needs for companionship and sexual relationship are involved, but the basic tasks to which a normal home offers itself. Who will love and care for the children—provide nourishment for their bodies, and guidance for their souls? Who will wash their clothes, make their lunches, take them to school or church or music lessons? Who will fulfill the role that is usually assumed by the mother in our culture?

Confronted with a variety of problems of this magnitude and, at the same time, struggling with the problems of his own grief and the dislocations that it brings into life, the widower is not in the best of positions to make the wise decisions that are essential for the welfare of his family and himself for the years ahead. This is the time when special help and counsel may be most needed, but it is more apt to be the time when criticism is most freely given.

Research, as well as common observation, make it clear that the widower is freer to act on his own behalf than the widow would be, generally speaking. At the same time that he is seeking to resolve his grief and reorganize his life, for example, he may also be trying to assess the personal qualifications and resources of another human upon whom he would thrust the most difficult of problems. He would be trying to find one who could help the children resolve a grief that they may be more apt to act out in behavior than express in words; so it would take someone with considerable insight to see clearly what is going on in the lives of children and at the same time establish a satisfying relationship with a grief-injured widower.

It is most unfortunate indeed when another human being is used to help resolve grief, for this involves identity confusion as well as active frustration. No two human beings are the same; they are the composite of all that has happened to them and all that has been invested in them by heredity and environment. They also have their own dynamic qualities. To expect any one person to replace another involves a vain hope. It is important for a person to work through grief before being in the position of establishing a fruitful relationship with another human being.

With the older widower, for whom companionship seems to be the more important necessity, there seems to be a better opportunity for finding another person to willingly share his life, since the number of widows and other unattached women is considerably greater than for men. The problem here, though, is that the older a person is the more deeply rooted are his habit patterns and personality traits. Two persons of advanced years are apt to present each other with problems of adjustment that may tax human ingenuity to the utmost.

In a culture in which life-styles and social security rules have an impact on human behavior, and where there exist forms of experimental living that seek solutions for problems of resolving grief and sexual behavior, it is difficult to predict what the future may hold.

The vulnerability of the widow in our culture presents one of the more difficult problems of social, personal, and sexual adjustment. Her role in the community is greatly called into question, for a major portion of her identity has been derived from her status as a wife and part of a couple. When her husband dies, she is faced with social, economic, and personal problems that tend to isolate her from the community in which she has traditionally functioned. Her male friends hesitate to be helpful lest their motives be misunderstood. The widow is not only apt to be in grief but to feel the dislocation of her social status. Her response may be overdependence or overaggression, and either of these stances may be misinterpreted.

As mentioned previously, Dr. Phyllis Silverman, in her study of widows done under the auspices of the community psychiatry program at Harvard Medical School, found that the death rate among widows the first year after the death of their husbands was 700 percent higher than that of other women in comparable age groups. A comparable study done in Wales produced the same statistical findings, thus showing it was not the unique cultural setting of Cambridge, Massachusetts, that determined the nature of the vulnerability. However, another finding was that those women who cared for their husbands at home during their final illness were only half as vulnerable as those who did not. It seems clear that the opportunity to confront the reality of the dying process and do some anticipatory grief work does have a way of reducing the impact when the death comes.

Other studies of widows done by the Foundation of Thanatology made it clear that the need for acting out feelings in a wide variety of ways is essential to working through the deep feelings of loss. Also, it is clear that the more it is possible to act out these feelings at the very beginning of the grief process, the more readily the period of readjustment is managed.

Geoffrey Gorer established the fact that the more ways a person acts out feelings, the more quickly feelings are resolved. In fact he made it clear that the old-fashioned and elaborate funeral process was more helpful than the streamlined funerals that are currently being recommended in England. What Gorer found to be true in England today is probably as true in the United States, though detailed studies still have to be made here.

The cultural role of the widow must be assessed in terms of the status she acquired previously as a wife and the meaning of the now fractured roles she plays in family, church, economy, and community.

Starting with the necessary economic adjustments that often must be made, it is quite obvious that their ramifications may touch all the rest of life. The widow who is obliged to sell her home and move into a small apartment often cuts off the roots of her relationship to a particular neighborhood and circle of friends; and often she sacrifices a relationship to a church in which she has friends and acquaintances who understand her problems. Her ties to her extended family (with its sustaining relationships) may become disorganized by the necessary move. This is especially true when the move involves some distance.

To face the necessity of multiple adjustments to a new community, church, and mode of living when in a state of despair or depression is so difficult that the healthful responses may be put off indefinitely. The effort needed to move toward new and strange people may seem to be too great. Thus it is not unusual for a widow to become lost as far as the important human relationships are concerned.

Sometimes the contributive factors to such dislocation may in themselves be minor, while their impacts are major. For instance, the widow may never have driven a car. She might have felt that it was never necessary to learn, for her husband was always there to go with her. The fact that he is dead now tends to immobilize the widow, and she may not be able to meet her deeper needs for church and community just because she is not able to come and go as she pleases.

The widow's efforts to seek companionship are often misunderstood, and too often the comments relating to it have a cruelty about them that adds to the already difficult human situation. As a result, a highly vulnerable group of persons in the community have their plights enlarged by the very persons who would normally be expected to provide healthful intervention and compassionate understanding.

Efforts are now being made to meet the needs of widows through "widow-to-widow" programs, small group processes in church and community, and special groups such as Compassionate Friends, FISH, and THEO organizations. The intention here is to provide the atmosphere wherein free and open discussion of thoughts and feelings can take place.

Often these are revolving groups in which the nucleus remains fixed but people come and go as their need dictates. In one such group that I supervised for a number of years, it was interesting to see how new relationships were established and how the group began to provide a center for emotional life. People would say things like: "I feel more at home with this group than any other I know"; "It seems I can talk about anything here and people understand"; or "I didn't think I was going to make it, but now I look forward to being with you all week."

There are significant and useful ways of confronting the special problems that widows have, and there are ways of meeting these problems with wisdom and grace—if the problem is clearly seen and the desire to resolve it is a major concern.

In order to understand the basic problems that develop when death and sexual deprivation come together, it is important to understand how the security system of an individual works. Deep within the individual there are needs that are dictated by nature, and some of the most powerful drives of life are related to these individual and racial impulses. To try to deny their existence is not apt to be profitable, for these drives are indirect and may reveal themselves in covert ways that may be more difficult to understand and manage. But to understand grief and human sexuality, it is important to explore the meaning of the endowment we possess.

In the Sermon on the Mount, Jesus confronted the basic drives of human nature and demonstrated how they might be spiritualized. He looked closely at hunger and thirst and pointed out that these essentially selfish drives could be used for creating righteousness. He looked at the powerful drives that compose lust and showed how they could be transformed into the basic devotion to human need that leads to true godliness. He looked at the threat to the security system of an individual that comes with the death of someone loved and explained how this could be used to build strength into life.

The dynamics of these deep emotions is related to a part of the brain that is so primitive it still tends to put self-defense ahead of reasoning processes in many instances. The portion of the brain entrusted with these essential life-frustrations is called the *diencephalon*. This primitive part of the brain is located where the spinal cord enters the thalmic region at the base of the brain. The thalmic region governs the autonomic, or automatic, and spontaneous activities for regulating body functions. The control of breathing and heartbeat are autonomic.

Diencephalic activity is fueled by powerful emotions, and the ability to act quickly in matters of self-defense is guaranteed by the essential security drives of life. When confronted with danger, we find that we often act first and think afterwards. Sometimes we are amazed at our ability to act under stress. It is reported facetiously that the fastest hundred yards ever run was not in an official race but in a chase involving a frightened person and an angry bull. It may well be that the high-jump record was established at the same time—when the frightened individual reached the fence.

The powerful emotions that produce diencephalic activity come about when there is an accumulation of stress that brings a person to the breaking point, or when there is intense pain that cannot be endured without flinching. We can do a simple test to see how this process works. Move your finger toward your eye and you will find that at a certain point an automatic control of muscles takes over and your eyelids close in a self-protective process.

If you eat something poisonous, your system will immediately be organized to send warning messages to your stomach and the senses that protect the approaches to it. This will be true for all the rest of your life. Some people are driven to drink by irrational responses to intolerable internal stress. When a child, they experienced hunger pains and cried out, and when something was shoved into their mouths they found relief. When in older years they have the internal stress and figuratively cry out, they find that self-initiated psychotherapy may be achieved by shoving a bottle in their mouths. The difference, of course, is that one is food and the other addictive poison; yet the irrational process is set in motion by needs that cannot be raised to the rational level for examination.

When stress is great or pain excruciating, the connections with the higher brain are released, and muscular and glandular reactions can take place without rational examination. This produces highly emotional responses that are not understood or easily controlled. A person will say, "I don't know what came over me." Often this powerful self-defensive drive produces behavior that is not in character for an individual, but it is done before it can be analyzed.

When two major drives of life come up against each other, as in the death of a spouse, it is not unusual for powerful diencephalic drives to be released. This may lead to behavior that may seem nonrational or even irrational, and it takes special understanding to appreciate what is going on and why. Often this type of understanding is found among professionally trained persons who can be objective about the behavior they observe. The untrained person is often unable to interpret this self-defensive behavior for what it is—a temporary and powerful response to life-threatening events.

This makes it important for all concerned to have some clear plan of action that can help those who are under this intense form of emotional stress. The acutely grieving person should be very kind and patient with himself. He should withhold important decisions until things have settled down a bit, he should be willing to accept help from others. Most importantly, he should withhold severe forms of self-judgment. Sometimes the periods of distress can last for many months. One woman, a trained clinical psychologist herself, said that it was two years before she withdrew from this period of acute emotional stress. She knew immediately when it happened though, because one morning she woke up and everything seemed different. It is not wise to try to impose rational judgments on these powerful drives that have their own integrity and can assert themselves no matter what else happens.

For those who are close to the bereaved widow or widower, it is important to be perceptive of what is happening at the emotional level. Criticism is to be withheld and, where it becomes possible to talk out feelings, an understanding attitude created. In this way, the deepest feelings can become compatible with the most rational insights. This may not happen quickly, so it is important to allow time and availability for the self-exploration that is necessary for movement toward adequate self-perception.

When the most powerful drives of the emotional life assert themselves, it is essential to know what is happening and why, and then to be prepared to assist the process of wise resolution.

12

Grief and Love

We mentioned in an earlier chapter that grief was the other side of the coin of love. Now it is important for us to examine in more depth just what we meant. To tell someone that they grieve because they love is not much comfort. The quest for perspective on grief demands that there be a deeper understanding of the processes that relate person to person; it is only with this understanding that the more discerning work of mourning can be done.

In contemporary English, there is a paucity of words to express the complex nature of love. We use that one overworked word to express a whole gamut of emotions, from the activities of film celebrities to the most profound form of self-giving relationship of the disciplined saints. No wonder it is difficult to bring into sharp focus the important feelings we would explore when the very word we would use has such indistinct and vapid meanings.

Perhaps the ancient Greeks can be of service to us here, for they possessed a richer and more precise vocabulary for the composite emotion we call love. The Greek word *eros* is related to sensual feelings. It is the basis, or root word, for our concept of eroticism. It deals with the deep and powerful feelings that can be expressed physically. The eros dimension of love is important because it is the focal point of all of the other aspects of love. When grief comes, it is related to the physical object upon which the love was focused. At first it is difficult to convince the bereaved person that there is anything else besides eros; for that which has been so basic to the sensory awareness is no longer there.

During the early stages of loss, the person in grief is most aware of the emptiness or loneliness that exists when the person who was perceived with sensory awareness is no longer able to be touched, listened to, or seen. When we listen to the comments of the person who has been recently bereaved, their speech is filled with the evidence of this dimension of their loss. They will say things like, "I just can't get used to it. A thousand times a day I start to say something and then realize that there is no one there to hear." Or, "When his favorite TV program comes on I want to call him"—"I keep setting the table with a place for him. I can't seem to get used to his not being here." Or, "Every afternoon at 5:15 I wait for the garage door to go up. I have done it for so many years I can't seem to stop."

Because the somatic portion of human experience is so constant, our sense of the real is centered in the physical. It takes time for the healthful work of mourning to modify this perception and make us realize that the things that are really important are not physical and the things that can never be taken away grow from our spiritual awareness.

The Greek word *phileo* is the root word we commonly employ in words like *philosophy* or *philosophical*. It has the connotation of appreciation for wisdom or knowledge. It tends to be less emotional than eros and more oriented toward mental activity. To call someone an Anglophile, for example, connotes appreciation for the English tradition and other British attributes, but no real sensual involvement.

When someone dies, it may take a while before a person can move through the sense of physical loss and thus regain an active appreciation of the mental or intellectual relations that continue to exert their influence on life. But after a while it may be observed that a bereaved person takes on some of the reasoning processes and convictions of the deceased. In fact, it is not unusual for the bereaved person to adopt some of the special interests and mental activities that characterized the dead person. For instance, he may begin to read the type of books that were of particular interest to the person who has died.

A third Greek word, *agape,* has a more spiritual connotation. The meaning is understood in a cosmic context. It adds to the emotional and the intellectual framework the perceptions that grow from an active relationship to Ultimate Reality, that is, from God-consciousness. The love of God may have some of the elements of the sensual and the intellectual. Devotion and worship may have strong overtones of relatedness. The concept of God may have a way of satisfying the mind, but the resonance of the human spirit to the Divine Spirit is something more. It is a cosmic kinship that gives the feeling one can never move beyond God's love and care. If God is concerned about the birds of the fields and the little animals of the earth and the flowers that bloom unseen, how much more must there be an active resonance and relationship between the spirit of the God-conscious individual and the God of which he is conscious.

When death comes and the more obvious relationships of life are shattered, it may become possible for a bereaved person to rediscover the ties that bind person to person in a sense of cosmic unity. The mystic is aware of the Presence of all of life and is never able to move beyond that sense of unity. When this sense of God's presence is everywhere, it certainly changes the perspective on the event of death; for even death is a part of the cosmic unity, and those who have died continue to have their unique place in the pattern of God. Agape is the awareness of this indestructible dimension of love. It may be the best form of surcease from the pains of acute grief and loss.

When death comes and makes its impact on the relationships that have been so much a part of the everyday life of people, it may take some time and effort to work toward the forms of loving understanding that are not affected by a biological or physical event such as death.

The all-encompassing love of God is related to all of the dimensions of human experience. The words of Giardano Bruno, "Out of this universe I cannot fall," speak of this security of spirit. When Whitehead speaks of religion as

116

being "at home in the universe," he is speaking of the quality of loving relationship that cannot be fractured. This is the true dimension of love.

The love that is basic to grief is the all-encompassing life-experience that touches body, emotions, mind, thought, and spirit. It is a mystical extension of the individual life into the cosmic dimension of all existence.

Love is the ultimate form of personalization. As Buber has expressed it, the "thing" relationships are the "it" form of encounter with other aspects of reality. But the "Thou" relationships have to do with the special beings who are able to respond because they have shared in the creative nature of God through their own God-consciousness. When we speak of the nature of God as personal, we speak of the energy forms that, with Whittier, we perceive as "warm, sweet, tender," or, as Jesus chose to personalize it, in terms of the Jewish respect for the father as the priestly being in the family context.

In psychological terms, we would speak of love as the achievement of an identity relationship with another. The object of the love becomes so close in thought, word, and deed that, in effect, the other becomes an extension of self. When something good happens to the object of love, we have a good feeling about it. When something unfortunate happens, we can feel the misfortune as if it were our own. When something devastating happens to the object of love, we too, feel devastated.

This devastation seems like the loss of a part of our own being. In fact, at the emotional level, that is just what it is. It is quite like an amputation, except that it is emotional rather than physical.

With that thought in mind, an imaginative psychologist at Brandeis University, Dr. Marianne Simmel, set out to discover all she could about amputations, with the idea that this would throw light on the nature of the equivalent emotional loss in grief. She interviewed young children who had lost a part of their bodies, some by a birth defect, some by early accidents. She found that they did not appear to be aware of the impact of the loss, for they had not lived long enough to integrate the use of the body part into their whole way of life.

The phantom-limb phenomenon is the neural response that continues to send messages and feel feelings even after the body part is no longer there. Dr. Simmel did not begin to find any of this response until she worked with people who had lost a fully integrated body part through some accidental means. Then and only then was the phantom-limb phenomenon observed in massive proportions.

Dr. Simmel found out several other things that illuminate the nature of grief. The extent of grief is apparently proportional to the degree to which the object of love has been woven into the texture of living. Also, if it is lost without warning, a person seems to be caught off-guard. He has not had a chance to take a defensive stance, and this makes the impact more devastating. The implication, therefore, is that grief is apt to be most intense when the love relationship is most completely integrated into life and the loss comes without warning. Dr. Simmel found also that those who refuse to face loss of a limb have a more difficult time adjusting to a prosthetic limb, while those who can accept the loss and even take a philosophical or humorous attitude toward it seem to be able to adapt more readily.

While we know that an amputation is not the same as a loss by death, there are some factors that are the same. The loss seems most severe when the love is most complete. Also, attitudes toward the loss have a bearing on how the experience is managed emotionally. It seems that the more open and honest the response to the loss, the more readily is the adjustment to it.

Erik Erikson explains that identity crises seem to develop around three major foci. One is the loss, or threat of loss, of someone important in one's life-pattern. Second is the injection into life of new and threatening persons and events. And third is the change in status or role relationship. It is quite clear that the loss through death of someone dearly loved brings all of these causes of identity crises together at one time.

Perhaps there is no more intense love relationship than

that which exists between a mother and her child. When the child is carried as a part of the mother's own being for nine months, there occurs an integration of life processes that is both most elemental and most advanced. Organic change modifies the mother's being physically and emotionally while at the same time anticipation directs her thought toward the hope-for future.

Should there be death at birth, the emotional needs of the mother become acute, and must be understood and properly met to avoid a long and painful period of adjustment that may have its impact on future pregnancies and attitudes.

This would be especially true of the mother who experiences the sudden-infant-crib-death syndrome. Here the love is intense, and the event is unpredicted; and the unprepared parents have a difficult time adjusting to their loss. Because the cause of crib death is so little understood, suspicion and recrimination are added to the sense of loss, and human relationships are stretched to the breaking point. It is a matter of record that one of the tragic aftermaths of this baffling form of infant death is that when the parents need each other most, they tend to let their suspicions and their grief drive them apart. The result can be separation or divorce.

Along with the privileges and blessing it brings into life, love carries a burden of responsibility. And with all love, there is bound to be some ambivalence. Usually the joys and privileges outweigh the burdens, but when grief brings its stress and pain to life, the burdens of love may outweigh the privileges. This is when things can be said and done that are difficult to understand or forget. It is particularly important, therefore, when under the stress of grief, to nourish love, and not to take it for granted.

When grief comes to life, it has a way of involving all there is of a person—body, mind, emotions, and spirit. There are times when the being responds unequally to the stress. The body may hold up, while the emotions give out. Or the emotions may be misdirected, so that there is a spiritual crisis. A person may lose faith at the time he needs it most.

When this disproportionate response affects life, there may

119

be a threat to selfhood. A person may turn against himself in self-judgment and recrimination. All love starts with self-love, a healthy attitude toward one's self. So it is particularly important in this time of stress to keep a clear perspective on one's self. Be kind to yourself, and you will be more able to be kind to others. Love is often made up of many small acts of consideration and kindness. Never is this more true than during those times that grief places its undue stress upon life.

When children lose their parents, they feel a threat to the basic security system of their lives. From early childhood, the parent is a symbol of protection, wise judgment, and never-faltering love and acceptance. When death comes to a parent, this backlog of love and trust is fractured. Even when the parents are old and have been failing for a long time, there are unaccountable feelings that come into the picture. Different kinds of love produce quite different forms of emotional response.

Sometimes the death of parents looses sibling rivalries that have long been suppressed or controlled. Sometimes they are not even understood to be what they are. Yet when the death of the parent comes, there may be stresses and conflicts felt among the offspring that involve some of the unfinished business of childhood. This is the last time there can be a contest to see who can be closest to the parent, and so the competition to be the important person in making decisions can produce conflict just when mutual support would be most desirable. The benefits of love and the burdens of love have to be understood in order to resolve these sibling rivalries when they arise. Understanding what is going on can be the best way of forestalling the damage that might be done by the emotional explosion of poorly guided feelings.

As there are many ways for expressing love, so there are many ways for expressing the other side of the coin—what we experience in grief. It may be that we can predict the nature and quality of the grief by understanding the quality of the love that has existed toward the person who has died.

If the love has been tinctured by fear and apprehension, as is sometimes the emotional quality felt toward rigid and authoritative parents, it would not be strange if this fear and apprehension were carried over into the grief response. If there was a great amount of dependency in the relationship, it would quite naturally follow that the bereaved person would show a dependency in the grief process. If there was a great basis of faith and understanding in the relationship, it would be quite natural for the undergirding faith to sustain the person in bereavement.

It is not a deep secret that there are healthy and unhealthy manifestations of the love relationship. Some persons are set free by love, and others are enslaved. Some persons are fulfilled in love, and others, because of their limited capacities for selfless love, are diminished. Some love moves toward jealousy, while other expressions of love manifest a deep understanding and acceptance of the object of love. When death comes, the emotions that have been developing throughout many years will continue to manifest themselves and determine the nature of the grief.

Wise and perceptive love can help to modify the quality of the grief that is felt. Recently, a young mother called me and said she wanted to talk about children and their grief. When we sat down to explore her interest, she pointed out that she had been told she had cancer and would probably have only a few months to live. She told about the impact this information had upon her. She had become so compulsive that she had mended all of the children's clothes and set about planning their futures as far as education and health needs were concerned. Then one day it came to her that it was even more important to try to help them prepare for the impact of her death on their lives. She wanted to act out her love for them by helping them understand the feelings she had for them and the fact that her dying was not abandonment.

An elderly man had a severe heart attack and suddenly was faced with some basic facts of life. He had always been the manager of affairs in the home. His wife was dependent on him and content with this dependency. But he was warned that in a few months he might have another heart attack that could be fatal. So he set about the task of carefully and slowly moving his wife into new forms of responsibility, so as to modify her long-established life-patterns. In a short while she was handling finances and making decisions that he had always made. Because he loved her and was concerned about her grief, he tried in advance to reduce some of the emotional responses she would experience. So when he died a year or so later, he left her with more competence and skill for managing her life.

True love wants to make the object of love as mature and as competent as possible. The more wisely people love, the more they want to stimulate personality growth toward its finest realization. It is also true that the grief that is experienced by those who contemplate their own deaths may show itself in efforts to help the objects of love grow toward greater maturity. Thus it would not involve the deceit that would conspire against reality to make people more vulnerable. Rather, it would seek to use the privileged time left to face honestly the impact of death and the need to grow in inner resources for meeting it.

It may be that the period of life immediately preceding death may be used to stimulate growth beyond the physical and towards the mental and spiritual, so that those spiritual things that can be preserved and appreciated and those things that are merely transitory and physical can be seen in their proper light. In this way, love can minister to the needs of the grief-stricken, and even death can be the instrument for growth in life and love.

13

Grief and Growth

Several years ago I was invited to share a seminar at a psychiatric hospital that had an extensive program in research and treatment. The subject that was assigned to me was the relationship of grief to growth. In the treatment center, they were well aware of the fact that the extreme psychic pain of grief and loss caused many people to suffer emotional breakdown and collapse. But it was equally obvious that more people met the crisis of their grief in such a way that they grew stronger and more mature because of it. They had discovered inner resources they could use to meet any future crises of life.

It was the objective of this seminar to explore what the resources might be that make it possible for people to grow through their grief rather than be destroyed by it. In this chapter we will try to assess the processes that are central to emotional growth and personal adequacy.

Life never stands still. The processes incidental to all organic activity are constant. Some clearly definable factors, and some mysterious ones, are operative in this constant process of adaptation and internal development.

On our farm, we have a row of maple trees that illustrate the mysterious processes of adaptation. Many years ago these trees were used as fence posts for the stringing of barbed wire around the pasture. Now, fifty or sixty years later, it is possible to look at those trees and observe the way the life process shows itself in adaptation. In some places, the trees fought against the barbed wire as a hostile agent, and here the trees have long and ugly scars that deface the bark and inner structure of the trees. In other places, there is quite a different form of adaptation. The barbed wire has been accepted and incorporated into the life of the tree. Where this happened, the barbed wire left no mark on the tree, and after all of these years, all that shows is the wire entering on one side and exiting at the other. It looks as if there has been a small hole bored through the tree and the wire carefully inserted.

When one walks along this long line of trees and sees some trees severely scarred and others showing no trace of the intruding wire, it is natural to wonder what makes the difference in the quality of a tree's response to injury. What was there in some trees that made them injure themselves by fighting against injury? What made it possible for other trees to be able to incorporate the injuring object and become master of the barbed wire rather than its victim?

Perhaps we have a parable here of the personal response to the things in life that could be injuring. What are the internal forces and conditions that make it possible to reduce the injuring factor to the vanishing point, rather than allowing them to distort and contort the rest of life? What is there in a person that makes it possible to transform grief into growth instead of allowing it to become a life-destroying intrusion into the forward progress of human development?

The dynamic factors in growth are constantly at work to modify life. To continue the analogy of the tree, it is possible to mark growth by the rings that develop each year as the tree matures. Persons with knowledge about trees can interpret the life history of a tree by examining the growth rings. They can tell the years of drought and the years of abundant rainfall. They can tell the year when lightning struck. Clearly marked in the growth rings is the personal history of the tree. The cumulative process of growth has experienced, responded to, and stored up all that happened to the tree as it lived through weather changes, accidental events, and environmental influences. All there was of life was recorded in its inner being.

So it is with people. The constant impact of environment, emotional crises, and interaction with persons and events is completely recorded in the growth rings of life. What causes the differences in response and determines whether these life-events will mar and scar life or will be made a part of a healthy process of incorporation and acceptance? Especially, how does this process work when the life-event is a grief experience? How can the scars be avoided and the event assimilated into the experience of growth?

Emotional growth develops from the way a person manages the separation-events of life. Wise grief-management is essentially an acquired skill in handling the deprivation experiences of life. If these are handled well, life moves confidently ahead into new and varied experience; but if there is fear and pain with each new confrontation, the process accumulates distress, and death becomes an overwhelming hazard.

While the analogy of the tree and the incorporation of all experience in the inner being has some usefulness for exploring how people grow, there is another way of looking at growth. It may be measured as a line on a graph in which each year of life is plotted against the growth of personal experience. The line may show that in some years the growth was rapid and healthy, while at other times there were blocks to growth, and life stood still or regressed. In the early years of life, the growth may be rapid, and then there may develop external circumstances that have a damaging impact of the child's life. These events may have such a detrimental effect that the scars will be evident all the rest of life.

Birth itself may be a deprivation experience. The child as developing fetus has had a comfortable and all-sustaining world of his own. But the process of growth causes problems, and the space becomes so cramped that there has to be a change if the development is to continue. This change—in the event of birth—can be painful, and the transformation in environment, traumatic also. The small and complete world of the uterus has to be exchanged for a noisy, cold, threatening world that has to be adjusted to. New skills have to be learned, like eating and responding to others. Growth itself can be threatening; for if growth had not compelled birth, the fetus might have lived on in insulated blessedness. The implication is that all growth threatens the secure past and invites major problems of adjustment.

Another deprivation experience that can be fraught with problems that may plague life for years to come is the experience of weaning. Here again the emotional experience is a movement away from the warm, satisfying relationship toward the cold, unrelated, and unsatisfying experience. Growth compels the change (since it would be unreasonable to remain at the breast for the rest of life), but the circumstances surrounding the change may cause anxiety and uncertainty. When weaning is abrupt and inconsiderate of the meaning of the change for the child, it can cause modifications of attitude deep within the child that may later produce apprehension over any change.

Some people indicate that apprehension about change, essentially the conservative stance toward life, may be related to the deep anxiety created during major stages of adaptation early in life. Politicians seem to be aware, consciously or unconsciously, of the power of emotions; for they know how easy it is to manipulate people by threatening their security and pointing out the hazards of change. In effect they say, "Vote for me, and I will protect you from the pain of growth or the necessity for facing new and threatening adjustments to life." The constant interplay of political processes is built around the conflict between the stimulus to growth and change and the fear of loss because of it. Growth implies moving into the unknown or insecure.

These early experiences of adaptation and change may be generalized to social growth—the fear of moving into new relationships and responsibilities. This may make it difficult for a child to face the changes that come with moving into a new community. Adults may continue to feel apprehension when obliged to face growth experiences. So the new job, the new school, the new church, and the new human relationship may be fraught with anxiety and unfocused fears.

If the first day of school was filled with anticipation and the new experience was properly prepared for, the new events were enjoyed and life moved ahead. If, on the other hand, there was a threat of separation from secure surroundings, and feelings of rejection and abandonment, the first day at school might have been so painful that it tainted other moves toward growth and adjustment.

But it is possible for changes that involve deprivation to be entered into with proper conditioning, healthful anticipation, and the motivation that can make the future good and its events a challenge. This would certainly influence the way a person would look toward the major change and deprivation that comes with the death of an important person in his life-pattern. One can grow toward the wise management of grief, as well as toward any other significant deprivation experience of life. Every deprivation is an invitation to develop new skills and opportunities for healthful growth.

Education at its best is a constant process of giving people the insight and information needed to grow into new competence for living. This is as true with the processes of informal and unconscious education as it is with the more carefully structured approaches of formal instruction.

A young child struggles against the forces of gravity when learning to walk. At first, balance is uncertain, and often the forces of gravity win and the child falls. But with time the child gains enough control over himself to be able to cooperate with gravity. It is then that the child learns the art of walking, which calls for falling forward exactly one limited and controlled step at a time. Then the force of gravity makes it possible for the child to achieve forward motion. Soon it is so natural a process that he is able to walk and run and engage in such highly specialized activity that the mastery of gravity serves life. At no point does a person repeal the laws of gravity. On occasion, a fall or minor injury reminds one that gravity is still at work. But the processes of informal education make it possible to wisely use the basic realities of nature rather than be perpetually injured by them.

An illustration of the more sophisticated forms of conscious education would be the art of learning to sail a boat. The wind is a constant, and its direction may vary considerably in direction and intensity. Learning to sail calls for an ability to work with the wind so that it becomes a servant rather than a master. The whole structure of a sailboat must be seen as a collection of pulleys and ropes designed to make adjustment to the wind possible. If the wind is light, more sail can be carried. If the wind is strong, the sail can be lessened as much as is safe. If the wind is moving in the direction you wish to go, you can go with the wind. But if there is a contrary wind, it takes a special knowledge of vectors and a skill in adaptability to tack back and forth so that you go in the direction you want.

Deprivation experiences are usually considered to be in the same nature of contrary winds or the force of gravity. We must learn to use them for our purposes, or we will fall or be blown off-course and end up injured or on the rocks. It is the development of the skills that use the realities of life for our own clearly defined purposes that marks the true end of education.

Viewed in that light, the fact of human mortality and the impact of death on life may be important parts of the growth of a person. Death might be considered a contrary wind. It can interrupt life and force it to go against its main purpose—unless a person learns how to use the experience for wise and consciously directed growth.

Benedictine monks spend some time each day in meditation about their own deaths. When asked the meaning of this form of meditation, they explain that it is necessary for one to look death honestly in the face in order to be able to live with the full awareness of the meaning of our mortal natures—both in terms of our ethical obligations and our spiritual possibilities. If we deny the limitations of life, we may ignore our obligation to each day as it comes. If we fail to prepare our inner beings for the responsibilities of each day, we may put off indefinitely the task of developing our inner beings and thus not reach a clear understanding of the relation of the finite to the infinite and the temporal to the eternal.

The forward movement of life is organized around the experiences of adaptation and cloture. We start a day with the necessity for planning its activities. At night we lay ourselves down for sleep with an awareness that it is an act of cloture for another of those parcels of life we call days.

The way we begin and end a day may well determine for us what the day produces. Often the day begins with the raucous sound of the alarm clock and ends with the nightcap that helps to chemically blot out the pain and anxiety of the day. How much wiser it would be if the day began with a time of meditation and prayer centered upon the values of life and the privileges of each new segment entrusted to us. This could change the content of the day, for we would be looking for different experiences during the day. Then at night we could relax and entrust our lives to a cosmic process that would bring peace deep within, and sound and healthful sleep as well.

What would be true of a day might also be true of the totality of life. In the language of Bryant's "Thanatopsis," just as we would prepare for each day and at its end seek inner peace, so with life we could value each segment and at the end "draw the draperies" of our couch about us and "lie down to pleasant dreams." We would have learned the ability to live with a "sustained and soothed" attitude that is nurtured by an "unfaltering trust."

Mozart was one of the great creative souls of musical history. He produced much in a limited span of years. The clue to his creativity may well be found in his attitude toward life and death. When his father was dying, Mozart wrote him a letter that illustrated this unfaltering trust. He said: "Since death (properly understood) is the true, ultimate purpose of life, I have for several years past made myself acquainted with this truest and best friend of mankind so that he has for me, not only nothing terrifying anymore, but much that is tranquilizing and consoling. And I thank God that He has bestowed on me the good fortune of providing the opportunity (you understand me) of recognizing death as the key to our true blessedness. I never lie down in my bed without reflecting that perhaps I (young as I am) shall never see another day; yet none of all who know me can say that I am socially melancholy or morose. For this blessing I daily thank my Creator and wish it from my heart for all my fellow man."

In the rich creativity of his own life Mozart seems to have found a way to move beyond the fear of death so as to live each day to the fullest. The fear of death was past, so the richness of life could be appreciated. He used the forces of life to nurture life and not to threaten it. The discovery he had made was so significant for him that he craved it for all mankind.

There seems to be within each of us an irrational fear of death that expresses itself in rejection of life. Our death-anxiety has an irrational quality about it. We fail to appreciate or protect life. We deliberately destroy our lungs, our digestive systems, and our bodies by various forms of self-abuse. If we take the Bible literally, we realize that we are all descended from Cain the murderer rather than from the quiet peaceful Abel whom Cain killed. Mythologically speaking, there is a deep impulse in man to act out his awareness of the burden of consciousness by deliberately or symbolically acting against his own best interests. Death-anxiety has a way of doing that. But there is a better way that can be learned. We do not have to destroy ourselves to confront our mortal natures. Rather, we can confront the meaning of our mortality by seeking to fully understand the privilege and purpose of life. Then we will be in a position to make each day so rich in its meaning that we can build upon it the eternal dimension of existence.

The concept of man's mortality is one of the basic facts of life we must learn to work with. Like the impact of gravity on the young child learning to walk or the influence of contrary winds on the person learning to sail, we cannot act as if we did not know its impact on our growth and learning. But we also know that there are some things we cannot experience until we have grown enough to master some important arts. Walking is an art of balance that cooperates with gravity. And untold aeons of time have been employed to develop the musculature and bodily adaptation that is necessary for walking. Men have long gone down to the sea in ships, and the skills of the mariner are the end product of adaptation to reality.

Learning to live with the fact of death is also part of the long-developed skills that emerged when man became a creature blessed and cursed with self-consciousness. Just as we cannot change ultimate reality, so we must learn to live with it so wisely that we can make use of adversity, rather than be destroyed by it.

One of the more refined arts of life is to learn how to live with both our mortal limitations and our immortal aspirations. When our fears and anxieties—generated by a preoccupation with our mortality—block out our awareness of the immortal, we are led to self-destruction and chaos. But when we learn to focus our attention on the values of the indestructible quality of our own natures, then we are prepared to live life with the awareness of its ultimate meaning and divine potential. Then even our grief and suffering can be a source of growth, and, given a proper perspective, it can make us more competent beings.

14

Grief and Self-Fulfillment

Perhaps our first question would be what is the difference between growth and self-fulfillment? If we grow through grief, what do we add by thinking of grief as a source of self-fulfillment? The answer of course is that all life is involved in growth, but not all of life is an experience of self-fulfillment. In this sense, what we will be considering in this chapter is the ultimate form of self-directed growth. For it is when the potential of the wise management of grief brings to life the perspective that simultaneously enriches life and teaches it self-mastery that the processes of self-realization and the achievement of the ultimate forms of self-awareness can occur.

Usually the task of religion is to view life and the incidents of life in such a way that self-realization is achieved even through pain and suffering. It centers about the effort to make the best out of the worst. The redemptive process works to turn defeat into victory. Basically, the processes of self-fulfillment take the endowment of mankind and lift it to its highest possible expression.

Religion works to set a person free from the ideas, the prejudices, and the small goals that can consume life. In the place of the littleness, it seeks to galvanize the resources of being that make it possible to achieve greatly even in the face of adversity. What we are thinking about, therefore, combines psychological insight, philosophical perspectives, and theological commitments to arrive at an inner state of being that masters life instead of being mastered by it.

Self-realization as a goal for living has been brought into focus in psychological thought by Abraham Maslow. It was the premise of Maslow that we had spent too much time trying to understand why people became troubled and disorganized and not enough in trying to understand why they were able to achieve greatly and master the events of life. He sought to understand what there was in man that could make him a master of life.

This quest for the something extra in man opened some doors that had been set ajar by previous thinkers. While the tradition of modern psychology had usually considered the stirrings of mind in the direction of spirit as basically only epiphenomena, William James, Henri Bergson, Carl Jung, and Gerald Heard sought to understand that something extra. Jung found that in the movement toward maturity, many persons had a second adolescence. The motivation and meaning of the first adolescence had been used up, and there was a need for a new concept of life and an adequate motivation for the next stages of growth. Bergson's vital spirit seemed to charge all of life in this quest for larger meaning, and James's concept of the true mysticism determined the framework for this development toward the ideals and drives that sought self-realization and self-fulfillment in a more compelling form.

The quest for meaning required that the basic questions of theological importance be answered again—this time from the point of view of the adult who was demanding more of life than there was to be found in the original and practical answers to these questions.

For instance, the basic question of identity, Who am I? must be reexamined. In the first adolescence it might have been sufficient to identify one's self in terms of occupational and marital expectations. But when success in career and marriage have been achieved, what more is there to life? How could a person perceive himself so that he could continue to have meaning for life after the original goals have been achieved? New and larger answers were necessary. A person needed to be more than a dentist or a husband or a parent. He needed to be seeking the meaning of the next stage in his personal evolution. He needed to be able to say in some way, "I am a being with spiritual needs and spiritual capacities that must be developed if I am to sustain the basic drive of life."

It is during this period of second adolescence that an individual begins to be preoccupied with his life and death. Is all of my quest for meaning to be outwitted by a biological event? Is death the final answer to all my striving and training? Must all of my efforts be in vain because death will be the final conqueror?

The ancient religious answer to this query of the second adolescence is that the soul of man is so unique that death cannot be the final answer. The self, with its capacity for consciousness, is the ultimate reality, and death is only the transitory event marked by the secondary reality of the space-time frame of reference.

In the contrast between Apollo and Dionysus, the former has to do with the rational—the requirement of dependability, law, and order. Apollo is related to the ideals of early Greek thought, the self that is disciplined and seeks to find the way in life through self-knowledge. Know your limits as a mortal being, and live within the rational framework of life. Avoid the sin of pride and the expectation of more than is available to a mortal creature. Avoid the error of *hubris* with its insolence and arrogance. Apollo would teach men the boundaries between the mortal and the immortal and help men to learn the fine art of living within their limitations.

Quite in contrast, Dionysus represents energy forms related to nature that stood in awe of the mysteries of life and sought to translate the mysteries into the powerful dynamics of his resonant nature. Dionysus dares to believe in the powers of his own mind and spirit. He wants to celebrate life not in terms of a discipline that adjusts to death but rather through the undisciplined assumptions that will not be satisfied with less than the unlimited claims his spirit will demand. So Dionysus becomes the wild God—man's most audacious assumptions about life. He is reflected in the exuberant excesses of life—the Saturnalias and Mardi Gras. The Dionysian way accepts the punishments that attend great risks because it believes in the worth of risk. "Man's highest good must be bought with a crime and paid for by the flood of grief and suffering which the offended deities visit upon the human race in its noble ambitions" (Nietzsche).

Every culture has some of both Apollo and Dionysus, just as every major religion has some of the qualities of these ancient Gods. We are invited to know the truth that will give us freedom at the same time that we are urged to give our devotion to one who claimed divine sonship and suffered the consequences upon a cross. Thus each life, deep within its struggle for meaning and identity, is faced with the decision as to whether it will observe the boundaries of an Apollonian compromise or be satisfied with nothing less than the sin of *hubris*, which assumes a status in the universe that places one among the gods.

What is true for an individual in his quest for identity is also true for the complicated assessment of social relations with all of their contributions to and expectations from life. Here the basic religious question has to do with the simply phrased question, Who are you? This is the question that is essential to marriage, to community life, and to social institutions. It is the question our Founding Fathers faced when they confronted the task of creating a new government. They came up with a Dionysian answer in the Declaration of Independence and said, "We hold these truths to be self-evident that all men are created equal and are endowed by their Creator ..." But some of the same Founding Fathers took the stand of the disciples of Apollo when they created the Constitution, which was an effort to structure life more practically.

The intensity of the relationship with the other persons in our lives determines the nature and quality of our grief. But it is possible to look at those we love and lose with an awareness that they, too, are not limited by their physical nature and are able to achieve dimensions of being that make it possible for them to claim undying qualities of being. When we are able to relate to these undying qualities, we are able to modify the impact of loss so that the preoccupation with the physical is kept in a perspective that also responds to the possibilities of the eternal. We can make the daring assumptions about the nature of the spirit and support it with the scientific verifications now available in physics and psychology (more about that in the next chapter).

Another one of the basic religious questions has to do with the value system of the individual that assesses life in terms of quality rather than quantity. In its simplest form, this question might be phrased, What am I? This immediately leads to distinctions that have ethical implications. Am I good or bad, wise or foolish, selfish or unselfish, loyal or disloyal? Some of the distinctions have social implications, such as, Am I a boy or a girl?—a question posed early in life that has lifelong impact—or, Am I rich or poor?—which has to do with role in society. Such queries directed toward the self tend to determine the value structure that operates in life consciously or unconsciously.

Questions having to do with the value theory of the individual tend to determine which of the varied reality systems of life will become important in determining how he will live, what is important in his life, and how he will assess the ultimates by which he measures life's relationships. These value judgments will relate to death and grief when they are phrased in questions like, Am I mortal or immortal? Can I feel confident in the ultimate spiritual value of my own nature? or, If when I am dead that's it, shouldn't I do it all now?

As you look at your own life and the lives of those who are important to you, your ethical judgments and theirs will help determine how you feel about death and how you will experience grief.

The last of these simple theological questions has to do with the purpose of life—Why am I? This query calls into question the nature of creation, the relation of the creature to the Creator, and the significance of the life-experience. As Viktor Frankl has pointed out, the central encounter of life develops at the point that ultimate meaning is assessed. If life has no meaning, then there is no meaning for death. But if life has great meaning, then the questions about the meaning of death become basic to the mental and emotional state of the mortal person.

If a person can answer the question about meaning with the feeling that his being has cosmic significance, that he is important to God, and that his struggle for values is not without meaning in the cosmic pattern, it will certainly have some important bearing on his sense of life's meaning and his basic relationship to the realities he creates and accepts.

It is quite obvious that these theological questions have to be answered with an awareness of the important realities that are determinant of ultimate values and personal assumptions. Self-fulfillment is determined by the nature of the ultimate reality that is employed in assessing life-experience and establishing the value system that governs life.

There are at least five different reality systems that can be the end result of the inventive-creative process in the life of an individual. The data assessed by the different systems, the experience evaluated by the differing realities, and the importance of the reality system for the living of life tend to determine the quality of self-fulfillment and the nature of the grief that is experienced.

There is a temporal or artificial reality created by the external value system of the society within which our lives develop. This reality is often unexamined, but its input into life is constant. For instance, it has to do with time, and our lives are often structured by time factors that say when we will eat breakfast, lunch, and dinner. This reality may vary from farm to city and from nation to nation, but it has an impact upon life, and many of us are caught up in its demands. Business, industry, education, even religion, may respond to the demands of an artificial, socially created reality, despite that reality's absence of rational foundation.

Another reality within which we constantly work involves the material fed into consciousness by our senses. This reality is basic to much of science and daily life. We say that seeing is believing. We live as if this were so. Yet we know that our sensory input is largely a response to physical things that may be easily distorted and cannot always be trusted. That is why we wear glasses and use hearing aids.

But the rules and regulations of life related to this frame of reference can be quite demanding, and if we make assumptions based on other forms of awareness, it may easily be called into question by those who ask, Can you prove it? And in terms of the question asked, it is usually sensory proof that is sought.

Yet we know that it is an inner process, electrochemical in nature, that is employed to determine the impact of sensory input. The ear is sensitized skin tissue that responds to air waves, just as the eye is highly refined skin tissue that responds to light vibrations. Something within the mental process of the individual translates these impulses into meaningful data for response. The eye of the artist sees more because his mental processes are more refined. The conductor of a symphony orchestra hears more because he has acquired skills in the differentiation of sound; he can discipline his responses to the raw sounds that others might interpret as noise.

The inner mental equipment that processes the data of sensory awareness is a center for judgment and values. It adds so much to the raw data of the senses that it determines the capacity of the moron versus the genius. It makes it clear that the essence of life is found, not in the data, but in the processing of the data. Self-fulfillment, then, has the qualities of a learned response to life.

But there is another reality that also must be taken into consideration, for the inventive-creative response can also be re-creative. The mental process not only responds to the date when it is produced by the sensory equipment; it can also recall it. We can hear music in our consciousness when there is no orchestra playing. We can close our eyes and see sights free of sensory stimulation. The reality of the system of recall, reorganization, and transcendent thought has its impact upon life; thus it can be essential to the higher forms of grief management. The refinements of consciousness make it possible to live well beyond the temporal or artificial input of life, just as life can move well beyond the data of the sensory responses. More than we realize, life is determined by the inventive-creative and the transpersonal processes that are constantly at work within our beings.

The person who can live increasingly in the inventive-creative reality and in the transpersonal or spiritual reality can bring the experience of grief into focus in realities of consciousness that are well beyond the time-space or physical frames of reference. This is where the cosmic response is enacted. This is where the pains of death are past and the transcendent perceptions transform the physical experience.

The mythic reality adds another dimension to the human experience. Every significant culture has developed its mythology. This is the social projection of ideals and meanings that are larger than the perceptions of the individual. Myths are restatements of the cultural ideals in their grandest form. The Greek's relation to the God he personalized through his mythologies brought a flavor to all of his life. The myths of the Gothic tradition were frozen into architecture and set to music and poetry by Goethe and Wagner. In the American tradition, myths found expression in the gigantic creatures of Aztec and Toltec literature. In more recent times Americans have created mythological dimensions for such heroes as Washington, Jefferson, and Lincoln.

Carl Jung has studied the significance of these impulses of various cultures to build the mythologies that bring to life daring assumptions about the human experience. He makes it clear that the human struggle against the anxieties of life and the fears of death may in part be resolved by the efforts to create the larger-than-life-sized products of a collective consciousness. By gathering up the cumulative experience of history, both social and personal, and restating it in a heroic form, each individual, in his own way, may share some of the heroism.

When the individual confronts death and the experience of grief, he may succumb to the cramped concepts of the temporal and sensory realities. He may not realize that there are other realities quite different but just as valid as the sensory one that can set him free from the destructive aspects of grief and give him the chance to assess life-experience in terms of the inventive-creative, the transcendent and spiritual, and the heroic claims of the great mythologies.

Self-fulfillment, as Maslow views it, is an achievement of inner climate that integrates life-experience, not in terms of reductionist perceptions centered about the sensory and the temporal, but in terms of a life free to confront life and death and thereby to add the glorious dimensions to consciousness.

Consciousness is the endowment that can take all of the input and data from the five realities and bring them together in perceptions that touch the depths of being at the same time that they create the visions of imagination. Imagination is sometimes derided as being unreal. But the human consciousness is constantly at work creating images that have an interpretive function for life. And the person may be free to create the more exalted images that can enlarge life, just as he can make the puny images that limit his capacity for self-realization.

The great religious questions that are confronted when we face life or death produce answers that are grounded in our willingness to live with the great reality systems rather than the artificial and reductionist systems, since the latter are bound to sensory data that can be very misleading. For the ultimate crises of life, the ultimate realities alone can suffice. The growth of the inner kingdom is essential to the self-fulfillment that comes from finding the right answers to the questions of life.

15

Grief and
Ideas of Immortality

One of the most audacious and persistent ideas generated by the mind of man has been a concept of his own immortality. In the earliest dawnings of history, sixty thousand years ago, there was a belief in life after death. In anthropological studies of our contemporary ancestors, there is also a deeply rooted sense of an undying spiritual dimension of life.

In our day, with reductionist science pervading the thoughts of many people, there has been the assumption that ideas of immortality are unwarranted superstitions grown from a misunderstanding of dreams or merely wishful thinking. A biological orientation would tend to assume that there would be nothing more than the biological. Those who see life as chemical action would easily assume that when organized life as we know it ends, no amount of hopeful claims could change the simple facts of life and death.

But the advanced science of our day offers some concepts that make alternative theories of life and death tenable. The scientist's concept of ultimate reality as extrasensory and transpersonal gives a new perspective to ancient assumptions. The nuclear physicist cannot depend on sensory input for information about the reality of the external world, for the infinitesimal particles are so small that they have never been seen and probably will always be beyond the reach of the limited sensory equipment with which man is endowed. But the reality of the unseen is verified by mathematical formulas and refined instrumentation that produce the evidence of what is, yet shall remain unseen.

And the particle concept of reality not only makes space difficult to fit into sensory perception but also makes time a largely untenable form of perception; for if the ultimate reality is bound up with the life of a particle whose life-span is a millionth of a second, we know that in this chain of reality it comes and goes before its existence can be registered on the limited equipment of our senses.

So science itself moves beyond the old measurements of reality. They can no longer serve a purpose in identifying the ultimately real. And now science has moved ahead to the extent that it must depend on the extrasensory and transpersonal to continue its explorations into the nature of the reality it dimly perceives.

But one thing becomes quite clear in moving from the science of Mr. Newton to the science of Dr. Einstein. Death was built into the Newtonian concept of reality, for it was space-time–oriented. An apple fell through space in an interval of time that was measurable, and it hit Mr. Newton on his head, which was able to feel and generate a physical and mental reaction. The death that was measured by space-time concepts was at home in Newtonian physics. But death has no place in the concept of a universe that moves beyond the relevance of space-time measurements. Change is the order of this new approach to reality, and the physicist speaks of the sixth dimension as an eternity dimension and has no apprehension about such an idea's undermining his system.

Much of the ancient thinking about immortality that has been bequeathed to us from biblical times originated in the Ptolemaic concept of the universe, which depicted the earth as a flat surface with an arched dome overhead and a place of hot springs and turbulence underneath. Thus it was easy to imagine a three-storied universe with a time sequence that intruded upon ideas of life and death. Death became simply an extension of life into an immortal state. This mood was transferred to the writings of Jesus' disciples, who knew no other concept of the universe, and thought of immortality as one person's going to prepare a place for faithful followers. These ideas persisted in the behavior of martyrs, who were willing to trade their mortal state for guaranteed immortality. But at best this reflected a cosmological idea untenable in our day.

A closer look at the revelation of Jesus reflects quite a different cosmological pattern that is much more compatible with contemporary cosmology. Perhaps we are the first century in history that has had an adequate scientific base for understanding the meaning of the revelation. Jesus kept emphasizing the quality of "is-ness." The eternal now was constantly showing through in his words and deeds. While his temporal and sensory life was lived in the realities to which they were attuned, his major revelation was related to the realities that were beyond the convenient measurements of space and time. The transfiguration moved beyond space and time. The spiritual realities were not bound by space and time. The relation with God was not in the past or the future but in the present, which was not space-time bound. In the prologue of John's Gospel it is clear that the reality of the revelation was not bound by time but by the limited concepts of time that were available. Nevertheless, the writer tried with them to point to the timeless quality of the revelation.

When we grasp the fact that the portion of God that is invested in each individual, the divine image, shows up in the integrative capacity of consciousness, we understand why this endowment, which can bring the realities together, has already achieved an immortal dimension. And as God could not be self-destructive, so the endowment of consciousness, which is the portion of God invested in man, cannot be destroyed. Man already has the mark of the infinite and the eternal, but the ability to grasp this fact of revelation is something that does not happen quickly and easily. It is, rather, the triumph of disciplined and refined consciousness.

The physical sciences (as they are expanded through modern physics and cosmology) make the idea of eternal life not only possible but essential to the system. But equally important is the fact that the personality sciences in our day are now hospitable to the idea that the consciousness of man is the ultimate focal point of creation and that in the course of understanding the meaning of consciousness, we understand also the meaning of life. And it naturally follows that as we gain insight into this idea of life, we also gain new perceptions about death.

A psychiatrist who experienced a transpersonal illumination wrote about it in depth of insight and enthusiasm in a book called *Cosmic Consciousness*. In this book, Dr. R. M. Bucke speaks of four levels of consciousness. To begin, there is simple consciousness, which we see among the higher animals. Then there is self-consciousness, which is essential to language, education, and a historical perspective and seems to be characteristic of mankind and his unique endowment. Third is cosmic consciousness, which is characterized by a resonance to the life and order of the universe and awareness of relationships and meanings far greater than that achieved in self-consciousness. Beyond this cosmic consciousness is a level of illumination that is probably quite rare, but is real to those who experience it. A total response to heightened consciousness, it brings to consciousness its highest awareness. Perception becomes inclusive rather than exclusive, and the unification that is traditionally a part of the mystic's vision is achieved.

Dr. Bucke feels that the content of our mental lives is continually being expanded and enriched and will eventually reach a point of fusion. Here an amalgamation of thought and feeling produce a new and exalted state of consciousness that raises man's potential to a new form of actualization. In his exploration of this experience he relates the origins of the great religions to this awareness of mystical dimensions of being; but he also points out that the demands upon man's consciousness become so great that often the response is to try to escape the responsibility that goes with it. Thus we have not only an evolution toward a higher spiritual state but also reactions against it. These are characterized by retreats into materialism and efforts to reduce life to less challenging and more comfortable dimensions.

When the consciousness develops to the extent that it can

feel secure with its great visions of the unity of all life and the validity of its high perceptions, it has prepared itself for the life that has no boundaries in space and time but is secure in its awareness of indestructible cosmic extension. What Dr. Bucke and his friend William James started has lain dormant for decades but is now coming to life again among those who find a new unity in the audacious assumptions of the physical, the biological, and the psychological sciences. The research carried on today quickly moves beyond the old and comfortable boundaries, and we have the contemporary equivalent of the scientific revolutions that emerged from the expanded awarenesses of Galileo, Milton, and Newton. The necessary reorganizing of philosophical and theological perspectives was painful then and is painful now. But the benefits of growth are not achieved easily.

The inventive-creative capacity of humanity emerges in a long and slow process. Human responses to color were limited in early experience, as is reflected in primitive literature. But with time and experience and refined capacities, the basic color perception was expanded from black and white to the major colors of the light spectrum and then into the unlimited variations that we now see in color charts and artwork.

What was true of the development of color sensitivity is also true of the developed sensitivity to sound. Musical history is relatively short, but the early Greek modes, or scales, have been enriched by ever new inventiveness, and the capacity for invention seems to have paralleled the ability to be sensitive to variations of sound and rhythmic forms. A magnificent symphony would have been an impossible achievement for those who had previously experienced nothing more than a simple melodic line. The collective development and the individual capacity have come together over many generations to produce the rich and varied quality of contemporary music.

We might say that the increased sensitivity to color and sound amounts to a transcendence of former capacities for perception. Pierre Tielhard de Chardin sees something comparable in man's spiritual development. From a

145

preoccupation with the simplistic and more primitive approaches to reality, man's capacity for consciousness expands into an awareness of his concept of a *Noosphere,* a spiritual perception of all reality.

With this combination of the new approach in the physical and psychological sciences, it becomes quite clear that the concepts of ultimate reality can undergird man's awareness of the eternal dimension in being. Perhaps there is nothing that can modify the impact of grief like the faith that can see the quality of life that is, in essence, transcendent, transpersonal, and spiritual. Such concepts can so undergird life that the experience of biological death comes to be perceived as incidental to the rest of life. The life-perception of the God-conscious being far surpasses the biology of the death-event.

Perhaps the finest resource for coping with loss and grief is the developed capacity to believe greatly about the nature of God, the nature of man, and the interrelationship between them that is able to develop the capacity for consciousness to its highest degree. Then the believing produces the altered states of consciousness that make spiritual perception so clear that all of the rest of experience in life falls into its proper place, that is, becomes the raw material out of which spirituality is created.

Our ability to believe in the eternal dimension of life, then, is dependent upon our capacity for developing our own inner kingdom. This requires two things—purity of heart and skill in meditation and prayer.

We are reminded that out of the heart come the issues of life—also, that a special grace comes to the pure of heart, for they are blessed with clear vision, cosmic perception, and face-to-face encounter with God.

There has long been a deeply felt assumption that the spiritual state of the individual has a bearing on the possibility of his achieving an extension of spiritual existence after the biological event of death. Some of the rather crude actions of the church in history have centered around this idea of earning or buying spiritual status in the sight of the church.

Crude ideas of a geographical heaven and hell and an intermediate state of purgatory have been part of the effort to interrelate assumptions of responsibility with the cosmic process. But the type of spiritual development we are now concerned with is not something that can be bought and sold, for cosmic bargaining confuses the realities. The limits of the temporal and sensory cannot be imposed upon the transpersonal and spiritual. The values that are created in the consciousness of an individual that have a right to cosmic status are the end results of disciplined personal achievement. Only with the contemporary understanding of the processes of consciousness have we moved beyond the outworn concepts of the crude consciousness in a crude universe.

When we see man's spiritual development as an achievement, we see his development of qualities of inner being that make it possible for him to be at home in the spiritual and transpersonal spheres of reality. It seems that it is only as this conscious being creates the conditions for spiritual life that the full promise of his spirituality becomes active in experience.

This achievement of a spiritual state that is at home in the realm of spiritual reality is not as strange as it seems. Just as primitive man had not developed the coordination and sensitivities that give color consciousness and musical awareness, so the person who in contemporary life has failed to develop the higher sensitivities tends to block out from his life many of the more rewarding experiences. When this happens at the spiritual level, it seems difficult, or impossible, for a person to live in a spiritual realm that he does not know exists. It is the struggle to become a spiritually mature and sensitive person within the bounds of time that makes it possible for this sensitivity to function beyond the bounds of space and time.

J. B. Rhine, after years of experimentation with the capacity of the mind to function beyond the man-made measurements of space and time, said that according to his own definitions, he had been able to verify the capacity of consciousness to achieve immortality. Basically, he was speaking of the ability to move beyond the limits of temporal and sensory reality so as to function in the extrasensory or spiritual and transpersonal spheres. By this observation, he was saying that it had become clear to contemporary psychology that the so-called audacious assumptions of spiritual beings throughout history were, in truth, based on valid assumptions about the nature of ultimate reality and man's relationship to it.

The disciplining of consciousness is now a matter of great interest in psychology and personality research. The phenomena of consciousness are now studied in depth, and it has been found clearly possible to alter and modify consciousness so that it becomes more resonant to the extrasensory and spiritual reality. This is what meditation and the spiritual disciplines are all about. The ancient mystics and the saints knew this from their experience. Contemporary humanist psychologists discover it in laboratory experiments and in the impact of meditation on organic function, psychological orientation, and personal adequacy.

The person in disciplined meditation seeks to use the capacities of the mind to organize the energies of being in order to produce the achievements of a higher consciousness. The mind brings into focus the symbols of the spiritual and dwells with them until they so dominate consciousness that the spiritual takes precedence over the other realities upon which the mind is apt to concentrate in daily activity. The objective is to use the capacity of consciousness for the ultimate achievement of consciousness. When this is done honestly with the self, purity of motive and heightened awareness of meanings may emerge. In fact, with devotion and skill, there may come the moments of spiritual illumination that are the finest achievement of the spiritual quest; for here the purified heart sees clearly into the nature of reality, and God's nature and purpose are seen as a personal revelation. As Henry Margenau, the Yale physicist, says, the mystic is able to peek through the keyhole of reality and see the truth.

When meditation achieves the purification of being, the

highest reaches of the meditative life are discovered. Man is at one with God, and the insight into the nature of being makes the artificial boundaries between the realities disappear. Consciousness then melds the separated realities into a new capacity for unity, and death is no longer a source of anxiety and fear. The truth of the resurrection becomes a personal experience, and one can look at physical death as if it were a minor aspect of a greater process of man's spiritual development toward the moment when the individual consciousness and the cosmic consciousness are one.

The fear of death and the sense of personal defeat that is basic to acute grief is washed away by the understanding of the spiritual dimension of being. While the personal experience of separation and loneliness may persist, if it is seen within the spiritual perspective, it will have quite a different impact upon life. Instead of being the final defeat in relationships that are purely biological and physical, it will be seen as the transition from one state of being to another, with no accompanying diminution of the essential quality of being.

Immortality, then, is not so much an extension in time having the prospects of restored relationship in some future event as it is a verification of the validity of the extrasensory, transpersonal, and spiritual realities that are already eternally existent in consciousness. We do not move beyond space and time by a manipulation of space and time, but rather by an achievement of spirituality that encompasses our space-time perceptions in a larger framework of reality.

Then, what we know, what we believe, and what we are will become an integral reality. We will know we cannot move beyond God's love and care because we are eternally immersed in it. And we will understand the natural processes of photosynthesis, metamorphosis, and resurrection in their eternal dimension. All of life will be sustained in the faith that creates and invents its greater grasp of reality.

16

Grief and
Crisis Management

Persons doing research on the impact of human crises upon the life of an individual have produced some important findings. For instance, in the course of psychosomatic medical research they have discovered that many physical illnesses appear to have their origin in some emotional crisis that has disturbed the body chemistry of a person on a chronic basis.

Also, they have found that these emotional crises have a cumulative impact. In fact, crisis psychologists have developed what they call HCUs, or "human crisis units." A human crisis unit is an effort to measure the stress that is placed on an individual by a life-event that is expected to have an unusual emotional impact.

Although there are several classifications of these events by different researchers, the general principle is clear. For instance, a serious illness may be allotted ten HCUs. The trauma of a divorce may be judged worth fifteen HCUs. When a child goes off to college, it may be worth only five HCUs. On most scales, the loss by death of a person important in your life rates highest in HCUs—twenty-five.

It is quite clear that these various separation-events in life have devastating impacts. Sometimes several of these emotionally distressing events come together all at once or one right after the other. This tends to place a cumulative burden on an individual. When the accumulation of stress is more than the person can handle, there may be some form of organic, emotional, or social breakdown.

Psychosomatic research has made it clear that many illnesses are organic responses to accumulated stress. The coping skills of the organism are overtaxed, and functional breakdown is one of the results. The emotions most immediately affect the glandular system, which controls the body chemistry. Body chemistry, when healthy, tends to check viral developments and abnormal cell division. When the body chemistry is thrown out of balance for long periods of time, the control mechanisms are modified, and viral infections can go out of control. In addition, abnormal cell division may run rampant. It is this condition to which attention is directed in the prevention and control of cancer. There may well be emotional factors involved in neoplastic tissue growth.

Most people have developed certain coping skills as they learn to make choices and live with consequences. Every choice involves a deprivation of some sort, but usually it is compensated by being able to choose a more desirable alternative. However, some of the events in life provide only a choice between undesirable alternatives, so that whatever choice is made, there is a stress and distress. The event of death often gives people a future that is weighted with undesirable alternatives. To live on in burdensome circumstances or move into an environment in which social relations are severely modified offers only a choice of stresses. Either choice will make demands on coping skills.

While we have become increasingly alerted to the impact of HCUs on the physical organism, we have been less aware of the psychological and social problems of adaptation to accumulated stress. Though people may feel themselves becoming weighted down more and more, and may realize that something is wrong, they may feel helpless to deal with their condition.

The adaptation to stress may show up in accumulated fatigue. This usually manifests itself in a weighted or burdened feeling. Everything is harder to do. Sometimes time weighs heavily on life, and at other times there seems to be too little time to do the things that need to be done.

Sometimes there is a pervading sense of confusion, as if it is impossible to see clearly what needs to be done. Other times it is a pervasive tiredness that keeps one from doing what is clearly perceived as necessary. Responsibilities pile up until it seems impossible to get out from under them.

Sometimes unmanageable stress is evidenced by a retreat from life. For example, there may be a reduction of social contacts. It becomes just too much trouble to get dressed and go to church, and excuses multiply to the extent that other people cannot be met and enjoyed. People say to themselves, "Nobody wants me around like this" or "They'll never miss me anyway" or "I'm just not up to it." So the content of social life is allowed to whither away and, with it, many of the resources that could help a person get through the hard places and reduce the stress that comes with high HCUs.

The depressive state tends to make life an inconceivable burden. The processes of depression tend to be cumulative, and the more a person retreats from life, the more reasons there seem to be to continue this backward action. Rational resources, impaired though they may be, tend to support the depressive response, so that the efforts to escape rather than confront the burdens of life seem self-justifying.

These varied negative responses to life, which we have briefly outlined as organic, psychological, and social, tend to be common responses to the accumulation of HCUs. But it is important for us to know that there are other and more valid ways of responding to the pressures and burdens of life. It is one thing to protect one's self from further stress by retreat, but it is quite a different thing to engage in the activities that can strengthen the resources of life so that the accumulation of crises can be met. In my book *Coping with the Crises in Your Life,* I surveyed in depth the positive approach to stress and the methods available for improving coping skills. Here, however, I will give but an outline résumé of some of the things that may be done to improve one's position in the face of life's HCUs.

In the first place, it should be made clear that when stress is great, it is important to be willing to accept help. When stress is placed on a bone, the bone may break. If the bone does break, there is need for special help in getting the bone set so that the inner healing processes can function properly. Most of us seem to recognize this need when what is at stake is a broken bone. But when it is a broken heart, we may not be as perceptive. We may not see clearly what the symptoms of distress are. A plaster cast speaks for itself. Changes in behavior, in attitude, and in health patterns do not announce themselves as clearly. When a person may most need understanding and support, he may instead be greeted with impatience, resentment, and rejection.

So it is important to properly interpret the cries for aid that may come from those suffering painful grief. The need for awareness must exist in individuals, in groups, and in institutions.

The individual who can provide help in crisis management may be a family member, a neighbor, or a colleague. Usually this person stands close enough to the bereaved individual to observe the signs of suffering. But sometimes the relationship is so close that the emotions of the potential helper are involved in such a way that feelings get in the way of wise understanding. This may be the case when there is shared grief. Then there may be impatience. That is when comments like, "So you're having a hard time, aren't we all?" and "What makes you think you're so special—we're all in this together" tend to reject the feelings of the person who tries to communicate pain in order to get help to relieve it.

It may well be that shared grief helps to create the understanding that is needed. Here it should be remembered that grief is a highly personal feeling and different persons express their grief in different ways. The important thing is not to try to mimic feelings or their expressions, but rather to recognize the right of each person to pour out his deep feelings in an atmosphere that accepts them for what they are—a personal matter—rather than rejecting them because they do not fit a preconceived notion as to how grief should be expressed.

What is true for individuals is just as true for groups. Life is lived in many group settings. The family is a group. The people with whom you worship, work, and play are groups. The purposes of many groups tend to predispose the type of response that will be made to the emotional crisis of one of its members. Often people report a loving, supportive attitude in church but a rejecting one at work. One study shows that the bereaved person is isolated, ostracized, and rejected at work. People tend to avoid the grief-stricken because they don't want to be asked to share another's burden.

When these conditions exist, it is important for the grieving person to recognize where help exists so that he can move toward it. Usually the family and church are more supportive than business and recreational groups, and the reasons are fairly clear. Group purposes tend to determine group actions. When the major purposes of groups move in one direction, it is difficult to change the group function to meet the special needs of one of its members.

It becomes clear that special groups with the stated purpose of helping the bereaved may be the most useful. A widows' group in a church or mental health center, a small group therapy session, or a spiritual life support group can speak to special needs with considerable usefulness because that is the reason for its existence. Its members share a common need and concern, and it gives its full attention to meeting the claims the individuals make upon the group.

Certain institutions exist to help people cope with life. The church, the therapy group, the rehabilitation group in a treatment center, all serve the common goals of strengthening coping skills so that people may be more adequate to meet the stress of life. These various resources of the community become the agencies that work to bind up wounds and relieve the stress of broken hearts until the normal healing processes have had a chance to take their course.

Also useful to the person generating crisis-management skills is having a good idea of what is happening deep inside him. At this point it should be clear that grief has a complicated and complicating impact on life. Self-understanding can make it possible for a grieving individual to be kind to himself and to accept changes in behavior and attitude because he understands that they may be the temporary responses to life stress.

Perhaps there is no more important time to be patient and understanding of ourselves and others than when we are in the grip of grief. This is when we can interpret our own needs so that we can seek help wisely. It is doubly injuring to seek help from those who will reject us. It is important to move toward those who personally and professionally can understand our need and can respond with patience and insight.

There may be no other time in life that it is so important to move into the texture of a supportive group life. It may well be that in these times of crisis, when our own coping skills are overtaxed, that we discover or rediscover the value and purpose of those institutions that exist primarily to enrich the inner resources for wise and healthful living.

Those who have studied HCUs intensively seem to believe that everyone has resources for meeting crises that can be trained and cultivated. These resources are emotional, spiritual, and intellectual. When they are needed the most, it is important for the individual to understand both his needs and the resources that are available to meet them. This, then, is where needs and resources come together to assure that the life-event will become a stimulus to growth rather than a cause of despair and personal disintegration.

17

Grief and Its Anticipation

People are highly vulnerable when they are caught off-guard. When major life-changes jump upon a person unannounced, the inner resources for adjustment may well be stretched to the breaking point. As we have seen in our exploration of the management of crises, there are some things that can be done to relieve the stress. One of the ways we can protect ourselves against the element of devastating surprise in life is to sharpen our ability to anticipate life's threatening experiences. In this way we cannot be caught completely unprepared for them.

How can we anticipate and prepare for life's distressing experiences? Well, when we stop to think of it, we are doing this all the time—whenever we want to avoid the possibility of our behavior having unpleasant consequences. For example, we study for our examinations so that we will not appear ignorant or suffer failure. We try to keep our muscles in good shape so that we can perform well in athletics. We try to anticipate the needs of our bodies through proper nutrition and regular medical checkups.

Yes, probably more than we realize, we invest much thought and energy preparing for the events that are inevitable parts of life. Even those things that could be considered tragic are hypothetically planned for. We insure our cars against the damage of collision. We insure our houses against fire and hurricane damage. But often these things are considered more of a precaution than a preparation for an inevitable event.

But as we pointed out in an earlier chapter, if you love someone, you become vulnerable, because their death could present you with an identity crisis of major proportions. Confronted with this inevitability of our mortality and our deep commitment to one another, we may try to avoid anticipation by putting such thoughts out of mind. Or we may say things will be different for us because "I will go first" or "Perhaps we will go together." The things we say to ourselves when we visit the lawyer to prepare our last will and testament reveal the varied ways we try to avoid the reality of our future.

Research has clearly indicated that people who are well prepared for a crisis seem to manage it better than those who are unprepared. Talking about, thinking about, and feeling about the future may be one of the best resources for coping wisely with what the future brings. But we know that anticipation can be either pleasant or disturbing. There is joy in anticipation of the good things of life, just as there may be anxiety in looking ahead to tragedy and suffering.

How can we use some of the same techniques of looking ahead to life's joyful events to soften the blows of unkind fate or accident?

What can be done to anticipate a feeling? Some researchers working with this problem say that it is impossible to "feel" a feeling before the emotional event that releases the feeling. The assumption here is that feelings have their own status and integrity and are separated from intellectual processes. They say that it is impossible to experience the impact of acute grief before the event that triggers that feeling-response. The implication of this theory is that people are largely helpless to take a defensive stance against the crisis produced by the death of someone important in their lives.

Others doing research on this matter say that there is important evidence to support the view that a chance to talk about an event and approach it with some awareness of its meaning can clearly reduce its impact. They find supportive evidence among people who have a close relationship with a dying patient, as compared with those who are kept at a distance. The facts seem to support the conclusion that moving through the experience of illness with a patient reduces the impact of acute grief at the time of death. When the death is sudden and unexpected, the bereaved person is caught off-balance and suffers the more severe emotional response.

Anticipation makes it possible for a person to maintain the forward motion of life. Somewhat like the person who rides a bicycle, it is difficult to maintain balance when the bicycle is standing still, but when forward motion is retained, it is possible for the cyclist to remain upright and control the forward motion of the wheels. When a person moves into a life crisis with enough forward momentum to help maintain stability, the crisis is managed more adequately.

It is quite true that the "forgotten feelings" of life are difficult to anticipate or recall, but it is equally true that all of life is so bound together that it is impossible to completely separate feelings and thoughts. We can learn to understand our feelings. We can interpret the meaning of the feelings that come over us. We can even be comfortable with the uncomfortable feelings if we know that they are not abnormal but are quite the expected response to certain life-events. In fact, we can even grow to the extent that we understand the value of the ill feelings and think it abnormal not to have a feeling-response compatible with the events that produced them.

What leads some people to feel caught off-guard is the absence of the self-understanding that responds to feelings as if they were valid and important parts of life. It would be a sad thing indeed to be separated from our feelings and thus be unable to appreciate them as essential to our wholeness as persons. While we may not be able to feel feelings in advance of the event that triggers them, we can understand the feelings when they occur, and we need not be threatened by what are normal and healthy responses to life.

In my book *Understanding Grief* there is a thorough exploration of normal, abnormal, and severely disturbed grief responses. Fortunately, most people respond well within normal ranges, even though they often assume their behavior is abnormal. How reassuring it can be to people going through this period to be able to translate their self-doubt into understanding. In itself, this can relieve some of the emotional stress.

Religion is an important factor in helping people live with a good grip on reality. As we have pointed out in earlier chapters, religion looks clearly at all of life, and recognizes its boundaries. It knows that death can be as natural as birth and that it has a quality of inevitability about it. This is part of a defensive stance. People with deep religious faith tend to be less threatened by the inevitable events of life because they have seen life and seen it whole.

Even when the events of life involve the destructive power of nature, as in the case of hurricanes, earthquakes, and shipwrecking storms at sea (where preparation for the unknown is difficult), it is possible to separate the raw power of natural forces from the divine intent that operates through the consciousness of man. Those who are wise understand it is the freedom of human nature that leads to vulnerability, not the ultimate will of God. In times of crisis, therefore, people are not separated from the supportive quality of their faith by false assumptions about the nature of God. To blame God for the life-destroying and grief-creating impact of an earthquake is to make it more difficult to gain a valid perspective of the reality of the relation of mankind to the forces of nature that one usually depends on for security in life.

The religious stance gives perspective on life—all of life, its joys and its sorrows. The religious stance seeks perspective on both the destructive forces that can be at work in the human experience and the resources that can be employed to meet the stress points of life.

We hear about the need for a defensive stance in driving our cars. This means that we are constantly alert to what may be around the next turn of the road, or to the possible errors of judgment on the part of those who share the highway with us. A comparable defensive stance can be adopted toward our

18

Grief and Its Resolution

It would be unreasonable to think that any emotion as devastating as acute grief could be quickly and easily resolved. The simple fact of the matter is that for many people the work of grieving continues for long periods of time or else goes unfinished. We need to realize this and to give ourselves and others some of the opportunities needed to work toward the final resolution of the grief as far as it is humanly possible.

Several studies have shown that grief experiences by young children in early life may be a conditioning factor for years to come. The feeling of abandonment that young children equate with grief may produce feelings of low self-esteem, and these feelings may impair normal and healthy life-activity for years to come. Violent reactions later in life that seem to have no clear connection with grief may be traced to death experiences and the emotional reactions that grew from those experiences.

Studies of vandalism have been related to hostile feelings against authority figures that are held responsible for the injustice of life. Even the behavior of some rapists is related to unresolved grief. Blind rage against women for a mother's abandonment through death demonstrates that the grief has never been properly interpreted or worked through by a child. Or it may show up in inverted form as an eternal quest for the perfect woman that tends to idealize all women and thus separate them from normal communication and relationships.

These unresolved grief-reactions among children may be paralleled by similar reactions among adolescents confronted with the death of a parent. These last may act out their grief in unwise experimentation with life and death. They may feel a burden of guilt that makes it difficult for them to cope with the normal responsibilities of life. It is often observed that their reactions may be so camouflaged that they are misinterpreted, thus crippling any effort to understand the reactions and help in the process of working them through.

Unresolved grief among adults may manifest itself in a variety of ways that affect life physically, mentally, and emotionally. The total life-experience of the bereaved person is involved in determining how he reacts to acute stress. If there is weakness in any area of life, the stress is apt to show up in that area of weakness. If it is a physical weakness, it may well surface as disease. If it is a weakness in social orientation, it may manifest as a withdrawal from social life or as hostility toward other people. If it is an emotional weakness, the stress may materialize in the form of emotional breakdown or maladaptive behavior of a psychological nature.

Let's look at some of the ways the unresolved grief or unfinished mourning process shows itself. The fact that the acting out is often unrecognized for what it is by both the bereaved person and observers may make the problem even more difficult to resolve.

Dr. S. was a competent physician who had a large private practice and important assignments in the local hospital. He was considered to be a completely competent individual and certainly one who should have had an awareness of what was going on in his own body.

Dr. S. had a fifteen-year-old son who became ill with a rapidly developing blood disorder. His father diagnosed the ailment and immediately provided the best medical treatment available, calling in specialists from distant medical centers. The medical intervention was to no avail, and in little more than a month the son was dead.

Dr. S. was overwhelmed with the loss and seemed to be doubly distressed because, as a physician, he felt he should have been able to do more than he did. He went on with his practice, but it was a heavy burden, and each week he seemed to feel more fatigued. About six months after his son's death, Dr. S. became aware of the symptoms of colitis. The condition worsened due to ulceration and the incident difficulties in treatment. Medical intervention relieved some of the symptoms, but the basic condition did not improve. When a biopsy finally showed a rapidly spreading cancer of the colon, the doctor gave up his practice.

It was at this point that Dr. S. made an appointment with a specialist working in the area of causative factors in the onset of cancer. For the first time Dr. S. talked freely about his feelings and his grief and his inability to cope with his sense of guilt as a physician who might have saved his son. He wept openly. He revealed that when he was fifteen, his father had died of a malignancy, and now he seemed to be inextricably caught between the anniversary events in his own life. His father's death and his son's death became in a sense the parentheses that held his life in an intolerable tension. It was only when he faced the meaning of these facts and the deep feelings that went with them that he began to gain some perspective on his own condition.

During the three months following his treatment by the specialist, Dr. S. experienced a remission of his symptoms, gained ten pounds that he had lost, returned to his practice, and appeared to have resolved the acute phase of his grief as it was manifesting itself physically. He continued to function quite normally until, some time later, he died of a heart attack.

Here in the case of Dr. S. we have an illustration of how the unfinished business of an old grief can compound a new one, often without a clear indication of the connection. The old wound was reopened, and the anniversary that tied the two events together made it doubly difficult to resolve the problem, even for a person who should have had a clear insight into the cause-effect factors involved.

It is important for us to be alerted to the possibility of a causal relationship between physical symptoms and the stress of unresolved grief, especially when there seems to be a clearly evident correlation in time.

It is also important for us to perceive changes in the social perceptions of individuals after acute grief, for they may act out the grief in nonrational behavior. This seemed to be the case with Dr. W., a professor at the local branch of the state university. He had always been known as a wise and well-balanced individual. His wife of forty-five years became ill and died after a long period of hospitalization. Prof. W. was disconsolate. He could not seem to put things back together. Relatives and friends tried to help, but nothing seemed to penetrate to where the pain was.

About two months after Mrs. W.'s death, a woman from a nearby town who had known both the professor and his wife came by with a cake. There was a long conversation, and in the next few weeks many more such times of sharing. Then, to the amazement of everyone, the professor announced his engagement to marry his friend. The family physician visited the professor and told him of the medical history of his bride to be. She had been mentally ill and had a long history of emotional instability. The minister visited the professor and tried to interest him in an exploration of his behavior. The family acted out their feelings of amazement and distress, and friends were slow to show their approval of the professor's plans.

It seemed that everyone but the professor recognized that he was trying to resolve his grief for his wife through a process that might not be healthful for either person involved. A deep commitment in a love relationship is quite a different thing from a desperate effort to resolve grief and fill up the lonely spot in life with another warm body. This form of unwise social acting out of feelings may intrude upon the life of a person in such a way that severe dislocation may occur. While it is wise and healthy to withdraw emotional capital invested in the life of the deceased person (so that it can be reinvested in fruitful living) it is quite another thing to try to use another person as a surrogate for the dead person and thus deny the need to resolve the deep grief and reorient life toward its more realistic goals.

Major changes in social behavior, especially when they are clearly out of character, may well be evidences of unhealthy efforts to do some of the unfinished work of grief.

This may also be true when we confront evidences of psychological problems that manifest as maladaptive behavior, neurotic symptoms, and loss of perspectives on life and its inner dynamics.

Normal neuroses are characterized by the difficulties in human relationships that occur when there is glandular imbalance in the system. Situational neuroses, which make it difficult for a person to function normally, may reveal themselves when there is temporary stress. The temporary neurotic patterns may be prolonged if there is an unwisely managed or poorly resolved grief process.

Karen was an unmarried woman who had cared for her mother for many years. She had never seemed to have any negative feelings about her life and enjoyed good employment relations in addition to her apparently good relations with her mother.

After Karen's mother died, there did not seem to be any serious change in her life at first. A stray cat came along, and she made a home for it. Then another came, and she did the same for it. These cats seemed to draw others—until Karen had more companionship than she really needed; yet she seemed unable to turn a cat away.

The landlord, who lived downstairs in the duplex house, was concerned about the cat population overhead. At first, he raised some questions, and then he raised some objections. Karen became more belligerent in her defense of her cats. She refused to let them go out for fear the landlord might injure them. She imported large quantities of kitty litter and, in small quantities, flushed it down the drain. The pipes became clogged, and she refused to let the landlord or the plumber come into her apartment.

Finally things became so difficult that Karen rented another apartment, where she lived herself, but went to her old apartment three times a day to care for her large family of cats. One day some of them were caught under the floorboards of an unfinished storage room and died, with disastrous results for the atmosphere.

Finally the landlord called the health department and registered a complaint. The representative of the health department broke into the apartment with an air purification mask over his face and reported that it was worse than the lion house at the zoo. The cats were taken to the shelter—all 118 of them—and Karen never returned to her former apartment again.

Various explanations of the behavior of this competent businesswoman were offered, but no one seemed to relate her odd behavior to the loss of her mother and the resulting emotional instability that made it impossible for her to avoid any imposition made on her by a living thing. Her neurotic behavior seemed to be a bizarre grief-response and needed to be treated as such.

It is important for us to be alert to the varied ways through which unresolved and unfinished grief shows itself. But it is even more important for us to make available the resources that can help grieving people understand both the obvious and obscure ways they may employ to resolve their deep feelings.

Again we mention that the funeral process may be the most easily accessible and healthful process for helping to do some of the unfinished work of mourning. Every time a person attends a funeral he is given an atmosphere for expressing deep feelings and seeking the support of those who understand and share his feelings.

Perhaps there is no better resource for working through the unresolved feelings of grief than to have professional counseling. Here is found the insight that can understand and interpret even the obscure behavior. Here is the wisdom that can strengthen the resources a person needs to get through the unfinished grief-work, so that the important tasks of life can be resumed.

Nothing can surpass the value of a creative faith that can see and understand the nature of grief and the value of the hope that springs eternal.

No one expects deep grief to be quickly resolved, but no one should have to experience the side-tracked emotions that can further disrupt life. Healthful grief can and should find healthful resolution, and the resources of religion, the community, and professional counselors should work to that end. Each of us in our own way can develop the discernment that will make it possible to help ourselves and others do the final and sometimes long drawn-out aspects of our grief work.

19

Grief and Your Life

We have looked at the human emotion of grief from many points of view. But for each of us, the most important part of any experience is what it means when it happens to us. In this concluding chapter, therefore, we will look at grief in the context of our personal experience.

A favorite theme of literature and the arts is the never-ending processes of nature that illustrate death and rebirth. Seedtime and harvest represent such processes. And in spring festivals, the rebirth of life, which has been submerged by the cold of winter, finds elaborate expression in the drama of Easter, with its promise of spiritual victory over the event of death.

Photosynthesis is basic to the life process, for leaves and other green things take light from the sun and carbon dioxide from the air and transform them into life-giving oxygen and the vegetable matter that abundantly supports most of the other forms of life on the face of the earth.

In the fall we watch the creepy, crawly things at work making their cocoons. There is little physical evidence that a transformation bringing new and beautiful life could take place. Yet the death of the caterpillar is essential to the life process. If we cut into the cocoon in the middle of winter, we would find only what appears to be a disorganized mass of loathsome looking animal matter. But beyond what we see there is a pattern and design working itself out, so that in the springtime the cocoon will break open and a creature of rare beauty will emerge. The butterfly or moth is evidence of a constant natural process that transforms death into life. The metamorphosis carries a promise that all there is is moving toward something not easily seen or verified by our senses or foreseen in our imagination. But with faith and patience the transformation takes place, and we can verify it.

No physical analogy fully satisfies our deeper emotional needs, for the grief we experience is more basic to our nature than any physical proof can satisfy. These metaphors of nature at best stimulate a faith that wants to believe what cannot be easily proved in spiritual terms.

From the New Testament we have word that the grain of wheat must fall to the earth before it can experience a new and manifold dimension of life. This we know of wheat and willingly accept. But what can wheat tell our aching hearts about the nature of a person and the relation of rebirth to the event of death we have so painfully known?

Perhaps we can find more useful analogies in the human experiences of death and rebirth that are constantly taking place in our living.

When we stop to think about it, we know that our everyday experience is heavily weighted with death and rebirth experiences. We have hopes that die and are reborn. We know the shattering of faith that is rebuilt stronger than before. We know the loves that have nourished life and then have withered away only to spring up anew in other places. Each of us in our own way has known the meaning of death and rebirth in our pilgrimage through life.

Often the death and rebirth experience is central to psychotherapy. A patient comes for counseling. After some time of exploration, it is often discovered that the forward motion of life is thwarted by some injury that has blocked life and growth. It might be a childhood experience that has made a person feel unloved or unworthy. It might have been some injury inflicted by a person who was trusted and then abused the trust. It might have been an unexpected hazard in life for which a person was unprepared and was caught so off-balance that things were never brought back into balance.

In the process of healing, it is often essential to confront and move beyond the experience that injured life and caused the death of a major feeling. Then it is necessary to discover what it is that is still alive and waiting to grow, so that the new development may be made possible. Sometimes it is painful to confront the various deaths that one has experienced with the kind of honesty that can set a person free to live again. But when it happens, it is as if a great burden has been lifted from life. The unfettered self is thereafter set free to grow.

Often the growth process is manifested in religion, where a small faith must die in order for a larger one to emerge. In adolescence, for example, one grows from the small dimensions of a faith that emerges from early instruction to confront the wonders of creation. It is not unusual for a youth to say that he can no longer believe in the God he was taught about in church school. What he is probably saying is that he has grown in his awareness of the creative processes in the universe and the old and small idea of God is no longer adequate to support his new adult faith. Sometimes the death of small gods is painful, but it is essential to growth. Emerson said that when half-gods go, the gods arrive.

Often when death occurs there are expressions of loss of faith. Persons say things that indicate their God is too small. They say, "Why would God do this to me?" or "I can't believe in a God who lets things like this happen." These are usually healthy statements. They denote a person who realizes that his perspective has been too small and that in order to cope with the tragedies of life he must develop a greater understanding of the law and order of the universe and the cause-effect factors that are constantly at work.

The tragedy is compounded when persons confront the need for growth in understanding and then run away from it. Then the pain of grief is increased, for the need for growth is ignored or rejected.

It is not uncommon for people to find a type of perverse satisfaction in their pain, as if it were in some way justified.

So when assaulted by personal dimensions of the life process, they retreat into a small and cramped faith that is inadquate for their needs, and gloat over the injustices and pains of life. This use of small perspectives as a counter-irritant for the pain of grief ill serves its purpose. The needs are too great to be satisfied by a retreat from life and growth.

The experience of death and rebirth must start within the self, move into human relations, and find its ultimate expression in the personal theology that relates the self to God as the ultimate source of wisdom and strength, energy and courage, in the life of any person.

When confronted by the major stresses of life—and grief is certainly one of the greatest of these—the individual must grow beyond the inadequacies that have been built into life by the times of carelessness and the failures of the growth process. The everyday occurrences of life ill serve the processes of growth, and often it takes a crisis to rid persons of trivial ideas and limited perspectives. The death of these inadequacies may well be found in the rebirth that comes with wisely managed grief.

Yesterday I visited with a woman who had gone through that personal experience of growth. As a minister's wife, she had shared the struggles, hopes and fears, failures and successes, of the parish ministry. She had the feeling that she and her husband had a close relationship to God and that because their lives seemed to have a built-in cosmic bargain, God would never let them down.

Then there came a frightful day when a sudden heart attack caused the death of the minister husband. The universe seemed to collapse. The personal pact with God seemed to have been violated by acts of cosmic carelessness and injustice. For many weeks a pastor friend stayed close to this wife, honestly confronting her anger, her feelings of abandonment, her loneliness, and her fears. She raised all of the basic questions. How was she going to raise four children who would be needing college in a year or two? How would she pull herself together to gain the courage to face the future? How would she find a home for her fractured family?

What could transform the dark and forbidding future to something beautiful and good?

Slowly, and as the inner timetable of her grief permitted, there was an open and honest exploration of her relationship to God and life. Her perspectives grew beyond that small and manipulative relationship with God and the universe that had been so much a part of her past life. She began to realize that there is no bargaining position with God. She faced the fact that it was not realistic to say, in effect, "If I promise to be good to you, dear God, will you promise to be good to me?"

Rather, this bereaved woman began to say to herself and to others, "As I bring my life into accord with the power and purpose of God, may I discover that deeper dependency that will work for good and help me to discover that in every death-experience there is also the possibility of a rebirth."

Now, four years after her personal crisis of bereavement, she had found a basis for personal growth that has given her the rebirth of faith and purpose she had needed. She has grown to be a more adequate and faith-filled person. In what came close to being a paraphrase of the Scriptures, she pointed out that the former things had passed away and a new and fuller life had been discovered. She said, "If anyone had told me this could happen, I would have denied it. But I have found a new and better faith. I have found a new love that in my middle years has a deeper dimension than I had ever known was possible. My family is together in spirit. Three are in college, and the fourth has another year of high school." As she went on explaining her new happiness, she was in effect giving witness to the fact of death and rebirth.

In New Testament terms, the human relationships that are fractured can be rebuilt and restored. The human experience of failure can be remedied by the effort to renew and enrich human bonds. In fact, Jesus made this mood of reconciliation a prerequisite to worship. If your brother has anything against you, first be reconciled, and then bring your gift to the altar. This is the process of death and rebirth in human encounter.

The experience of grief fractures relationships on another and more profound level, for the restoration of the physical is impossible. But the spiritual bonds of life are more significant than the physical, and the confrontation of death openly and honestly may stimulate the growth experience that makes God seem closer and more real—an embodiment of the spiritual that is essential to the rebirth of life and hope.

Richard Strauss, in his composition *Death and Transfiguration*, gives musical expression to this basic impulse of life to find, even in death, a meaning capable of nourishing the highest aspirations of life. Gustave Mahler, in his heroic *Resurrection Symphony*, makes another statement of this mystical affirmation, that is, the courage of the human soul to find its own rebirth at a higher level of understanding through each of its encounters with suffering, failure, and death. What has been stated so well in the universal language of music is being constantly reaffirmed in human experience.

The "amazing grace" of which we sing is in one way or another an affirmation of the ever-recurring opportunities of life to renew itself, to move beyond failure, to grow through trial and pain to new perspectives and greater faith.

Circumstance may condition our personal experience of growth, but our responsibility for the way we face life is both a privilege and a challenge. We are the key persons in the shaping of our destinies. We can use our painful experiences as excuses for retreating from life into the extensions of death into all of life. Or we can accept the promises of resurrection and rebirth and cooperate with the cosmic forces that are constantly nurturing the creative, inventive, and forward-moving processes of life. When all is said and done, we hold the keys to our own future. With faith and God's sustaining presence, we can grow through death to the wonders of our own rebirth.